JUN 1 1998

Problems and Solutions

PROBLEMS AND SOLUTIONS

A Guide to Psychotherapy
for the Beginning Psychotherapist

MARTIN KANTOR

PRAEGER

New York
Westport, Connecticut
London

Library of Congress Cataloging-in-Publication Data

Kantor, Martin.
    Problems and solutions : a guide to psychotherapy for the
beginning psychotherapist / Martin Kantor.
        p.   cm.
    ISBN 0–275–93490–X (alk. paper)
    1. Psychotherapy.   I. Title.
    [DNLM: 1. Psychotherapy.   WM 420 K165p]
    RC480.5.K355   1990
    616.89′14—dc20
    DNLM/DLC
    for Library of Congress   89–72198

Library of Congress Catalog Card Number: 89–72198
ISBN: 0-275-93490-X

First published in 1990

Praeger Publishers, One Madison Avenue, New York, NY 10010
An imprint of Greenwood Publishing Group, Inc.

Printed in the United States of America

The paper used in this book complies with the
Permanent Paper Standard issued by the National
Information Standards Organization (Z39.48-1984).

10 9 8 7 6 5 4 3 2 1

To M. E. C.

Contents

Part I
General Problems

Chapter 1

Introduction

This text takes an eclectic and pragmatic middle ground to avoid the Scylla of overabstractness and the Charybdis of overconcreteness.

OVERABSTRACT SCYLLA

Scylla is that dry and detached academic presentation that leaves the student with a mastery of basic theory, often psychodynamic, and basic technique, often analytically oriented, but with little real sense of how to run a psychotherapy session. Such presentations overlook how the patient expects, not a narcissistic, pyrotechnical display, but help with his or her problems. Such presentations encourage the therapist to focus on an internally consistent theory that can disregard the present plight of the patient. They may even imply that such immediately useful offerings as good advice, or pressure-relieving environmental manipulation, interferes with or is antithetical to the "real" process of therapy, relegating such direct assistance to "asides," typically called parameters. Perhaps permitted only after the session is over, these asides can then be distinguished from the "real work of therapy." Scylla presentations are overgeneral, overexpanded textbook chapters that limit themselves to defining psychotherapy, listing without evaluating the different psychotherapeutic techniques, contrasting psychotherapy with other modalities such as pharmacotherapy, and identifying good/bad qualities for the therapist to possess. They avoid editorializing, rarely citing helpful, wasteful (ineffective), and harmful therapist-patient interactions. They are safe but sorry.

OVERCONCRETE CHARYBDIS

This is the text that teaches an idiosyncratic approach. Idiosyncratic approaches are acceptable when suitable for one type of patient (e.g., grief), useful for one diagnostic category (e.g., schizophrenia), or capable of effective implementation in the hands of a limited number of therapists (often those who have special talents or personality attributes). They become unacceptable when inappropriately deemed applicable for all therapists and patients regardless of type, circumstance, and, in the case of patients, diagnosis.

A Classification of Idiosyncratic Approaches

One-sided Approaches

Sometimes the approach is idiosyncratic because it advocates the use of only one out of many possible psychotherapeutic techniques. Such an approach overlooks useful, appropriate alternatives, or actually belittles them. Examples include behavioral approaches that neglect insight, or the reverse, insightful understanding without necessary behavioral modification (such as practice to make perfect, or coercion).

Trivial Approaches

Sometimes the approach is not merely one-sided but also excessively trivial, so obvious that the patient has tried it already (and failed) or others without special training have already thought to suggest it to the patient. An example is "Try to relax." Another example involves the belief that exposure and reexposure to an early trauma will necessarily create mastery, not further trauma. The patient is forced into health by being trapped at the source of the trauma and asked to "relive it, this time with assistance." When used injudiciously or with the wrong patient, the patient quakes before the prompt yet fails to develop the equivalent of a tachyphylaxis of the spirit and grow accustomed to it.

Common to these techniques is the embellishing of pop psychology, through clever packaging, with a special, and unwarranted, luster.

Approaches Created from Concrete Thinking

Here theories are created by thinking not creatively but concretely. While concrete thinking can create useful theory or useful treatment approaches by accident, theories created this way often amount to little more than primitive witchery. An example is therapy based on the belief in magic, such as the belief in the power of wishing to make it so. The therapist may shout at the delusional patient much like the native tries to make the foreigner understand by speaking loudly, not clearly. Or the therapist may try to force a patient into health by encouraging him or her to "cut it out"—for example, shaking the patient like one shakes a broken radio to get it to work (misused shock treatment).

Approaches Created from False Premises

Other therapies are ineffective or dangerous because they are elaborations of quite tenuously true or completely untrue assertions, either overt or covert (e.g., "Diagnosis does not matter"; "Dreams are random products without meaning" or "There is no importance to unconscious processes." Like delusional beliefs these therapies may seem valid because they are valid elaborations of what are, however, invalid initial premises.

BETWEEN SCYLLA AND CHARYBDIS

Our aim is for a desirable middle ground between two undesirable extremes: inherently consistent, smugly self-satisfying, theoretically sound, but often therapeutically empty and/or ineffective theory, on the one hand, and, on the other, seemingly practical techniques whose impressive and persuasive wrappings belie their limited or occasional therapeutic worth—especially when overdependent for their success on the personality of their originator.

To this end two means are employed: (1) seven fundamental eclectic and pragmatic assumptions and (2) a problem-solution orientation.

Seven Fundamental Eclectic and Pragmatic Assumptions

1. There is an equilibrium between theory and practice. It is believed that both theory and practice matter equally, that good practice rests upon sound theory, and that sound theory in turn originates from good practice.

2. Much ore contains some precious metal. All schools of psychological theory and psychotherapy, no matter how seemingly trivial, bizarre, or excessively arcane, potentially contribute both to our understanding of the patient's normal and pathological behavior and to our understanding of ways to treat the patient. Thus we look to various schools for the solution to the patient's problem. We ask the question, "How can we best treat a patient with a phobia?" and look to analysis, cognitive therapy, or behavioral techniques, among others, for a good solution—good techniques, not the only technique or techniques—techniques, in other words, with more advantages than disadvantages.

3. Though there is a variable relationship between diagnosis and treatment, in part because diagnosis is only one criterion for determining treatment, and because, in part, other criteria, such as severity of disorder and psychological mindedness, are also important, some diagnoses do suggest specific treatments, others narrow the field of treatment possibilities, and still others offer relative or absolute contraindications. Thus acute mania suggests pharmacotherapy, be-

havioral therapy seems inappropriate for acute paranoia, and uncovering approaches seem relatively contraindicated for both acute and chronic schizophrenia.

4. Different schools of medical/psychiatric/psychological thought are often different in name only. The same psychological problem appears to, and is recognized by, practitioners of all schools. But what the internist calls stubbornness the psychiatrist or psychologist calls resistance. Of course, the same behavior takes on different costumes in different settings. For example, resistance will appear to the psychopharmacologist as a refusal to take one's medication, while it will appear to the analyst as a resistance to the transference. Different terms given to the same phenomena (*recidivism, transference resistance*) obscure the similarities between the phenomena.

5. Psychotherapies that appear different are more alike than not. Differences that seem momentous are often no more significant than the different approaches of the dermatologist, who starts with the skin and works his or her way back to the internal organs, and the approach of the internist, who starts with the internal organs and works his or her way out to the skin.

6. There is more than one way to treat an illness. Just as internists and surgeons can advocate different approaches, both potentially useful, both potentially curative, psychotherapists have more than one effective way to positively influence pathological behavior. The positive results are more than enough justification for the means.

7. Patients are people. Some texts of psychotherapy are missing a third dimension—the practical, included here. In this text problems are presented that other texts consider less than lofty, or even mundane. A problem with psychiatric diagnosis and description of therapy is that it often resolutely bowdlerizes the patient's fantasy and behavior, the therapist's response, and so the therapeutic process, by scrubbing it for presentation, resolutely changing the feel and context of the original. What a silly thing to do! This approach overlooks some of the most important information that presents itself to us. Rarely discussed, for example, is the issue of eating and drinking during sessions. What do we do with the patient who chews gum or who drinks coffee, slathering it down when we are trying to hear or wasting time in treatment with bag, cup, sugar, spoon, and napkin? Can this behavior be useful diagnostically? Does it tell us something about the patient's interaction with us—for example, is it a resistance? Should it be bypassed, or should it be interpreted? (Sullivan [1954] was only partly correct when he asserted, "everyone is much more simply human than otherwise." In fact, also true is how we are all more simply animal as well. Certainly psychotherapy is the arena to observe, study, and interpret our less lofty, less civilized behaviors as well as those filtered through intrapsychic and social gauze.)

In a related matter, it may be said that we have based this text on the principle of "do as I do, not as I say." We have found that the public statements of "The Revered" are often an unreliable indication of actual practice. Thus a well-known analyst spoke in public of analyzing negative transference, but in private, he allowed as how, during a session, he arose from his chair, went to the foot of the couch, stared and shook his finger at the patient, and told him, "If you don't stop this, I will throw you out." Where is this written?

Problem and Solution Orientation

Specific Problems

Therapists, regardless of orientation, have many of the same problems with their patients. For example, all therapists, whether analytically or behaviorally oriented, must deal with resistance. This text enumerates some of these problems faced by all therapists.

Specific Solutions

1. There is a special emphasis on adaptability. In keeping with an atheoretical basis—a wish to remain free as much as possible from the undue influence of one school of thought—the solutions suggested here are either possible in, or easily modifiable to, the different psychotherapies. Thus Appropriate Advice (a solution to more problems than some of us believe) may be given by both the analytically and the behaviorally oriented psychotherapist, though in different guises, or with different "languages" or "voices."

2. There is a special emphasis on what to and what not to say.

a. What to say: We include solutions in the form of actual responses to be given to the patient. These suggested responses are not merely general, theoretical gems, or highfalutin, excessively holy responses, often inappropriate for patients who predictably have real, earthy, human difficulties; not only are the problems selected for discussion more practical and realistic than those selected by most textbooks of psychotherapy, but the student is given, not general, but word-by-word advice in plain English about what to say and when to say it.

b. What not to say: Furthermore, and considered just as important, we do not assume that the therapist is a benign creature merely in need of instruction. Rather, we assume that all of us doing therapy have a malignant side to us, stemming from inherent ignorance, learned ignorance, or even malice. So it is assumed that the student will not only make errors but even unconsciously wish to harm the patient. For this reason pains are taken to tell or warn the student what not to say, when not to say it, and specifically advise him or her not only how to avoid self-embarrassment and wasting time but also how to avoid actually doing harm.

3. There is a special emphasis on handling specific symptoms. The patient who appears for treatment usually comes, not to "get analyzed" or "have behavior therapy," but to get rid of troublesome symptoms. We suggest specific ways on how such symptoms as delusions, hallucinations, obsessionalism, and phobic anxiety might be handled.

4. There is a special emphasis on handling resistance. Because the patient who comes for help also wants to keep the problems, resistances to treatment arise. Special sections are devoted to methods for handling these resistances.

5. Because transference and countertransference responses (defined elsewhere) appear to either facilitate or inhibit most forms of treatment, special sections are included that deal with transference and countertransference. We differ from other writers in our emphasis on countertransference over transference, not the other way around. In other texts transference, believed to be a "sin" of the patient, seems to be discussed if not more often than at least more honestly than countertransference, believed to be a "sin" of the therapist. We tend to expose our patients more than ourselves, for we seem to be, understandably, motivated not toward self-exposure but toward covering feet of clay with the magic slippers of infallibility, often believed to be superhuman.

IN CONCLUSION

In this text, written in as popular a style as is consistent with the nature of its subject, the student is encouraged to use simple English to help the patient. Simple English commands, suggestions, and interpretations, when correct and precise, can be no less eloquent and have no less precise and meaningful an effect than that of the effect produced by the surgeon with a scalpel. The therapist who is most direct, most open, and most clear with the patient will have the most dramatic, powerful, emotional as well as intellectual, positive effect. The mumbo-jumbo therapist, no matter how impressive, will fail, often resoundingly.

REFERENCE

Sullivan, Harry Stack. *The Interpersonal Theory of Psychiatry*. New York: W. W. Norton, 1953, p. 32.

Chapter 2

On Being a Beginner

The relationship between student and supervisor is often marred by excessive formality, embarrassment, and partisanship.

1. Formality. Routine, standard, conservative answers are given even to intelligent, inspired, creative questions.

2. Embarrassment. Most therapists, beginning or otherwise, are afraid to admit they are human, especially when they sense potential conflicts between their humanity and their work. They would like to ask, "Can I get angry with a patient?" or "What do I do if I feel sexual feelings toward a patient?" but they do not. They are ashamed to admit these feelings, ashamed to admit they have a body, and ashamed to admit what are normal instincts, instead believing them to be imperfections. (As a group, mental health professionals can be too permissive with their patients, too unpermissive with themselves.)

3. Partisanship. The need to avoid offending peers, loyalty to and identification with former professors, and sibling and Oedipal (intergenerational) rivalry with practitioners of competing schools of thought lead therapists to attack other schools as ineffective, silly, morally wrong, and/or dangerous. The beginner, even when his or her questions are not criticisms of or attacks on authority hidden beneath the polite cloak of wanting to know, is afraid to break ranks and risk accusations of inappropriateness or treason, even expulsion, by asking such questions as

"Is it proper to manipulate a patient to do one's will, for example, by reverse psychology? Are there adverse consequences?"

"What about giving the analytic patient advice? Drugs?"

"In cases of successful symptom removal by behavior therapy, will symptom substitution, perhaps worse than before, follow?"

We are not referring to the beginner's advocacy of techniques such as the primal scream, which, purported to be psychotherapeutic, are only crudely psychological, hardly therapeutic, and often ineffective or dangerous. (Even so, the beginner asks, "Then why are there not more adverse reactions than we see? Where are the patients reporting adverse effects from these psychotherapies"?) We are referring to such practical and useful techniques as naive approaches advocated in the lay literature (e.g., popular magazines); underground techniques that represent a body of sometimes useful technical knowledge passed from therapist to therapist but not acknowledged in formal discussion or literature; techniques once widely accepted but now out of favor; and techniques advocated by groups without political clout or academic imprimatur. An example of the latter is the existential interpretation of a female patient's drawing of a snake piercing the sun—a picture, for her less symbolic of sexual intercourse, than of a wish to enter the womb, where the patient might feel safe and secure.

Partisanship is, however, misguided when, like paranoia, its tenets are derived from a false initial premise cleverly manipulated to create a persuasive but false theory. (For example, Millon [1981] believes this to be true for one study of psychopaths.)

A STUDENT'S BILL OF RIGHTS

The student has a right to expect the following:

1. Neutrality. Expect an atmosphere in which you can ask questions of theory and practice without shame, fear of criticism, or fear of being belittled. Expect direct, meaningful answers.

2. Equality. The supervisor is not your parent. He or she must not treat you like a bad, upstart, Oedipal challenger. Even when your questions are rivalrous Oedipal assaults, they should be treated as questions and should be answered.

3. Psychotherapy. Some is appropriate when you have problems that effect your work. (Some problems that effect your life can be handled, too.) When problems are extensive, a referral for individual psychotherapy can be made—as long as the referral is not to a punitive therapist in the moral employ of the supervisor. (In one case a supervisor referred a supervisee for an illness he identified as one that prevented the supervisee from adequately discharging his duties, when in fact the supervisee was, in a healthy fashion, protesting poor working conditions.)

4. Confidentiality. Your privileged material should not be put into written evaluations, used to brand you as neurotic or emotionally ill and not discussed with administration unless it poses a direct threat to the patient's well-being. (As an example, discussion was appropriate when a patient was being seduced by his homosexual therapist on clinic territory and clinic time.)

5. Indulgence, patience, and kindness. Your lack of knowledge should be treated as a part of your immaturity, not as a sign of your ignorance. The supervisor will remember that he or she was a student at one time. The supervisor asked silly questions, made many mistakes, even semifatal, and even did a degree of harm to some patients. If not, he or she might have been too conservative.

6. Open-mindedness and eclecticism. The supervisor does not know it all and does not have all the answers. If the supervisor believes he or she does know it all and has all the answers, it may be a primary delusion ("I know it's so because I know it's so.") Too often what is considered to be basic theory or good therapy really means "that in which I believe," or that propounded by the supervisor's husband, wife, publisher, referral source, or currently favored guru.

Expect your supervisor, if not to have a thorough grounding in all the disciplines, at least not to show a prejudice against dynamic approaches, to believe dynamics are invariably conjecture without proof. If your supervisor believes that an organic cause has been found for all behavior, not just some behavior, supplement him or her with another supervisor.

7. Support. Your supervisor should encourage your growth and creativity, not suppress your spontaneity, talent, or genius. This is destructive to you, to the field, and eventually to the patient. The supervisor should remember that the beginner who seems to say, I know better than you, may in fact know better.

8. Understanding. For example, the beginner who proposes an outlandish form of treatment may do so not because he or she is outlandish but because the beginner knows or is in treatment with an outlandish therapist, with whom he or she has identified in a healthy fashion. One student many years ago heard of a therapy that he had no way of knowing was not accepted practice. He advised a schizophrenic patient to "scream to be free," not because he himself was incompetent or crazy, but because he was doing the same thing therapists he knew and admired were doing. Yet this student was branded as 'bizarre' without exploration of the reason for his seemingly bizarre but, at least in spirit, appropriate behavior.

9. Respect. Personal styles, individual beliefs, and personal sexual orientation should be respected.

10. Discipline. A too-softhearted supervisor does not teach as well as one who is tough and demanding. Your supervisor should insist on perfect work now, even though its implementation might take years of study and practice. He or she should insist that you read. Few mental health professionals read enough; they get too much of their science from news reports. They believe

incorrectly that the classics are outdated. They say there is nothing really new being said. This may be so, but at least the newer variations can be interesting and instructive.

REFERENCE

Millon, Theodore. *Disorders of Personality*. New York: Wiley-Interscience. 1981.

Chapter 3

Selection of Patients for Treatment

The beginning therapist caricatures patients by differentiating them into good and bad, often according to the following, questionable criteria.

GOOD PATIENT

Some therapists believe a good patient to be one who
1. is a presentable-looking young person;
2. makes an appointment in advance (not asking for one for the same day);
3. has a well-paying job with good insurance coverage;
4. has a job that permits him or her to come during the day instead of having to come on nights and weekends;
5. comes regularly, rarely or never canceling, or if canceling, gives proper notice;
6. never calls between appointments, and does not have emergencies that wake the therapist up at night or bother him or her on weekends;
7. comes early for the scheduled appointment (but not so early that he or she meets the patient with the earlier appointment in the waiting room or interrupts the therapist's presession nap);
8. speaks spontaneously at the beginning of the session;

9. speaks quietly so as not to be overheard by the next patient waiting in the waiting room;

10. works hard in treatment;

11. listens to what the therapist has to say, without argument;

12. is rarely or never loud, angry, rude, or abusive;

13. presents a discrete, emotional problem in a comprehensible, coherent fashion, and with good insight;

14. has a problem of recent origin but not one so acute that it cannot wait or so transient that it disappears almost as soon as therapy begins;

15. has a problem severe enough to be grist for the mill but not so severe that it makes the patient overly clinging and dependent, or requires hospitalization;

16. has a neurosis, not a psychosis or a personality disorder;

17. does not present a suicidal or homicidal risk;

18. does not act up, act in, or act out. Any acting-in or acting-out behaviors are moderate in severity, encapsulated, and the product of illness, not ill-will. An example of acting-in behavior that is the product of illness is found in the patient who appeared two hours late for a session. He was delayed because he was an obsessive-compulsive who, try as he might to get to the office on time, could not leave the house because he was unable to stop washing his hands;

19. pays session by session or promptly—within fifteen days of getting the bill;

20. improves or is cured;

21. shows his or her appreciation, not by silent testimony, but with thanks openly expressed, then, after leaving therapy, refers new, similarly good patients to the therapist.

BAD PATIENT

A bad patient is believed to be

1. hostile and preoccupied with negative transference. An example is the obsessional patient who made the therapist both the subject and object of his obsessions when, over and over, he alluded to an incident over which the therapist lost patience with him. Less objectionable are patients who are hostile at the beginning of the session then become tame, docile, and cooperative toward the middle and end of the session. More objectionable are patients who continue to be angry throughout, becoming virtually an adversary by the end of the session;

2. suspicious. This is not the highly suspicious patient who is basically realistic about why he or she is in the office and who really knows what is being done and how. It is the patient who is delusional about the therapist, for example, believing him- or herself to be a victim, a guinea pig, or an object of sexual derision or desire;

3. demeaning. The patient who demeans the therapist might view the therapist as an incompetent or as an underling, for example, an indentured servant, there

to cater to his or her whims. Sometimes by complaining to the therapist's superiors, such a patient turns therapy into a prolonged self-defense of the therapist;

4. entitled. This is the patient who misuses his or her rights as a patient to continue maladaptive behavior and/or avoid its consequences. Such a patient might deliberately provoke the therapist, then say, "You can't get angry with me; therapists aren't supposed to get angry with their patients. And you can't report me to the authorities either; this is all confidential";

5. selfish. Selfish behaviors are egocentric behaviors that are the product of ill will, not of illness. Examples are calling at night because it is more convenient than calling during the day; when it suits their schedule, appearing late, canceling at the last minute, or not appearing and not canceling; and not paying on time, or ever;

6. desperate. The patient may be without funds or reliant on insurance reimbursement, invariably delayed. Or he or she may have overwhelming real problems, either from bad luck or self-created.

Solution A: Look for the satisfactory, not for the ideal, patient. Do not condemn patients who are not "all good" as "all bad." Remember: most patients can benefit from treatment; and most patients can teach the therapist something new.

THE SATISFACTORY PATIENT

This composite constitutes the satisfactory patient:

1. Meets some but not all of the criteria for the "good" patient yet some but not all of the criteria for the "bad" patient.

2. Basically appreciates and uses treatment.

3. Has a bit of insight, not necessarily a lot. The patient with even a modicum of insight usually has enough to be treatable. Indeed, most beginning patients have but embryonic insight. Because insight is not a fixed attribute but can evolve with encouragement, all that is really needed is awareness of at least one of the following: vague anxiety and depression; a kind of mindless rigidity and inflexibility of attitude; excessive unreasonableness; the existence of repetitive self-defeating patterns; the inability to achieve as much pleasure as desired; the inability to achieve and/or accept success; excessive hostility to others; an inability to love (sometimes attributed to narcissism); and loneliness often attributed to an inability to make or keep relationships, especially when accompanied by awareness that the patient either fails to attract others through fault of his or her own or compulsively drives others away even when he or she wishes to hold on and maintain the relationship.

When somatic problems are incorrectly attributed to physical causes, the presence of the patient in the therapist's office is often indication enough of belief in the intrapsychic and intrapersonal—that is, emotional—origin of the physical problems.

4. Has subjective and objective problems requiring treatment. Make a list following this outline:

a. Subjective

(1) Symptoms. Include negative symptoms such as the inability to enjoy oneself when it is a sign of depression.

(2) Existential problems. Not the manifestation of a depression, these philosophical dilemmas often appear as considered unhappiness with oneself, one's fate, one's past accomplishments, and one's future potential.

(3) Behavioral problems. These are subjective when noted by the patient, objective when noted by others (often from different perspectives). They include sins of omission as well as sins of commission.

b. Objective

(1) Negative evaluations of and complaints about the patient. (Just because a problem is first presented by others, not the patient, does not mean it is not treatable. The patient may quickly adopt it as his or her own.)

(2) Emotional problems detected on psychological tests.

(3) Medical problems with emotional consequences such as thyrotoxicosis.

(4) Organic mental problems. The nonmedical therapist will make special note of the functional underlay and overlay of the organic problems. By *underlay* is meant emotional problems that worsen the organic, as depression worsens Alzheimer's disease. By *overlay* is meant the emotional response to the medical problems, for example, catastrophic response to awareness of loss of memory in the patient with Alzheimer's disease.

5. Comes and pays regularly most of the time, though sometimes forgets a session, or walks out of the office, check still in pocket.

6. Pulls back, gains control, and apologizes after becoming highly emotional, irascible, even openly angry.

7. Resists and acts out minimally.

8. Improves and is grateful but sometimes fails to give thanks, and often takes all of the credit or assigns it to lovers, friends, or natural causes.

9. Wishes to keep you for him- or herself, so refers patients, if at all, to your competition.

Solution B: Face reality and be practical.

FACING REALITY AND BEING PRACTICAL

The realistic, practical therapist expands his or her tolerance and/or field of interest. This therapist strikes a compromise between having a quickly filled busy practice full of difficult patients and waiting for the right/desirable/rewarding/easy/remunerative patient while hours are empty.

This said, while compromises are necessary in the beginning when the therapist is trying to establish a practice, the beginning therapist is cautioned not to fill his or her practice with too many difficult patients. Too many difficult patients will exhaust the therapist, drain the therapist's energy, make coming to work seem a chore, tip the schedule to all early mornings and evenings (with a dead space in between), and, if too many patients pay less than the established fee, create financial hardship.

The practical, realistic therapist (using verbal techniques) might have the following credo:

I will try to treat all patients who are needy, come voluntarily or are forced to come, want to talk, are willing to pay, have at least rudimentary insight (described above), and have treatable problems.

The following two rules are often helpful in being realistic and practical: (1) Since many "easy" patients work and can come only after business hours, accept difficult patients for the during-the-day doldrums. The knowledge that these patients are helping the therapist by filling up difficult-to-fill daytime hours will make the patient seem more welcome, and so seem less difficult. (2) Convert the difficult to the easy patient using the vehicle of the positive relationship. Patients in a positive relationship will often abandon their difficult behaviors, often the product of anger and disappointment, "out of love" for a therapist who, despite limitations, is sincere and tries to help.

ON SCREENING PATIENTS

Screening Patients over the Telephone

Most therapists do not have a receptionist and so do their own screening. Screening consists of two parts: finding out if this is a suitable therapy patient for you, and finding out if you are the one best suited for the patient. The therapist inquires about the patient's schedule and obtains a capsule summary of the patient's problem. Should the problem be emergent (suicide, homicide, decompensation), act the part of the good samaritan and do what you can to help the patient. Refer the individual to an emergency room if indicated, or call the police. (There are medicolegal considerations beyond the scope of this text.)

Note the following potential problems:

1. Some patients act out by demanding an appointment immediately, others by not protesting when they are placed on a slow-moving waiting list.

2. There are patients who say too little to be properly screened. Among these are paranoid patients who fear their conversation would not be kept confidential, is being overheard, or is being monitored.

3. Some patients call, not to make an appointment, but to muse about whether or not they are sick and need a therapist and/or to discuss their problems over the phone, unburdening themselves by, for example, confessing a sin.

4. There are those who call, not for themselves, but for a family member or friend, either wanting to make an appointment for them or wanting reassurance that they do not have a worrisome problem. (Problems are entailed in making

an appointment for another person, and it is difficult enough to make clinical decisions over the phone, let alone about a caller's relative.)

If you choose to see the patient, agree only to a consultation to see if the two of you are compatible. Do not commit yourself to being the patient's therapist or to a type of treatment (e.g., pharmacotherapy for panic attacks), and never make a promise of cure. The therapist who is uncertain may respond with a diversionary maneuver. The therapist who is hesitant about taking the patient on might suggest that he or she will call back, but only if setting an appointment is going to be feasible. The therapist who is certain that the patient is unsuitable for him or her but suitable for another therapist, or the therapist who is unable to accept the patient for reasons other than suitability (such as a full schedule) may volunteer a referral, especially when asked. Some therapists prefer to give the patient not one but three names. This gives the patient a wider choice and allows the therapist leeway should things not go well.

Chapter 4

Detection and Diagnosis of Emotional Disorder

To detect and diagnose the emotional disorder is the problem at hand.

In this chapter we discuss two among the many helpful approaches: detecting the presence of emotional disorder by looking for its warning signs (some of which are listed below) and diagnosing emotional disorder by determining the mental status.

THE WARNING SIGNS

Introduction

The following are warning signs to alert the beginner to the possible presence of emotional problems. They are detected primarily through informed intuition. They do not represent formal criteria readily amenable to scientific inquiry. They may or may not suggest a diagnosis. A search for warning signs should not replace the more formal diagnostic approach of the mental status evaluation (see "Some Warning Signs").

Often these warning signs are benign, that is, when found in the absence of other, confirmatory evidence, they represent normal behavior and its variations or transient problems not to be confused with a fixed, serious disorder.

Some Warning Signs

1. Anger proneness. The anger is inappropriate to the circumstances. It is grossly disproportionate to the triggering irritant or is irrational. Some patients are really hate-filled, as in the case of the patient who expressed her anger with the staff by putting her thorazine tablets in their coffee water.

2. Absence of overt anger. Patients may be reluctant to admit to feeling anger. Instead they remain on edge. They often describe how they feel "just ready to explode," as if they are "seething," or "turning green." Their outward behavior may exhibit sulking, haranguing, withholding, defying—that is, a passive-aggressive expression of anger. Or they lapse into remoteness, withdrawal, or taciturnity.

Overt anger may be absent because it has been introjected—expressed internally instead of at others. This introjected anger is covert, difficult to identify, and easily denied. When asked, "Are you angry with me?" patients may reply, "Not really, I'm just upset about something," or, "I'm angry with myself." Sometimes the anger-prone patient opens up, has an outburst, and attacks others, losing friends and even loved ones. These outbursts may be rationalized as the inevitable breakdown of controls due to an unremitting succession of provocations. The victim is likely to be perceived as its cause.

Note: Angry outbursts alone do not provide a diagnosis of an affective disorder. Paranoid, obsessional, impulsive, hypomanic, depressed, and cyclothymic patients all may have angry outbursts (with different content).

3. Fondness for sly baiting. Patients who provoke by (a) promising more than they can deliver (usually in a teasing way), (b) withholding, (c) depriving others of what they need after deliberately whetting the appetite, or (d) blaming others for their reactions instead of blaming themselves for their misbehavior are often acting out impulses of an aggressive nature.

A patient's unfaithful husband called his paramour from the home phone. Each month the wife saw the phone bill with the woman's number on it and understandably exploded. Rather than apologizing, the husband told the wife, "If it bothers you so, why do you open up the phone bill?"

4. Sadism. Many symptoms have a sadistic component. For example, grandiose patients demean others, while ritualistic obsessionals torture others. One patient tortured his wife by lining up all the objects in the living room in the same direction, returning them to alignment whenever she moved them about; another patient tortured her husband by insisting he put away washed dishes at the bottom of the stack so that the dishes would be rotated.

Each disorder has special sadistic behavior. The schizotypal patient may make us dread contact by the patient's bizarreness, the paranoid patient attacks with his or her suspiciousness, the passive patient attacks with passivity or ineffectiveness; the depressed patient attacks by being slow or "draggy"; the obsessive patient attacks by control or repetition; and the hysterical patient attacks with expressed or implied envy or competitiveness, or by teasing.

5. Criticism. Actions or attitudes of others are interpreted in a consistently unfavorable light. You cannot win with people who respond in this way. If you are pleasant to them, you are humoring them, but if you remain neutral, you are being distant.

6. Emotional extremes. The patient is too intense and emotional or too detached and unemotional. The patient is either too euphoric, or too depressed.

7. Contagion. Patients may be so anxious that they contaminate everybody with their anxiety, so phobic that they scare others, so obsessional that others begin to worry, too, or depressed enough to spread gloom.

8. Incapacity for simple pleasure. The patient is unable to have any fun. Always there is an excuse. "I am too tired / anxious / phobic / depressed / worried."

9. Negativity. What is meant here is the abnormally high incidence of "un" words negating positive qualities that crop up in studies of many patients: *unkind, unfaithful, unappealing, unapproachable, ungracious, unresponsive,* and *unappreciative.*

10. Unrealistic self-assessment. Patients treat themselves either too well (narcissism) or too shabbily (depression), indulging in grandiose self-congratulation when none is in order or in depressive failure to give themselves credit or acknowledge their worthiness to be loved.

11. Past orientation. There is a tendency to live in the past with too little input from the here and now.

12. Unrealistic expectations of others. An example is the patient who feels entitled now because of being spoiled as a child.

13. Dereism (unreality). Rational thinking is replaced with irrational thinking, realistic thinking by unrealistic thinking.

14. Sly, self-serving illogic. For example, paranoid and psychopathic patients are especially adept at sophistry. They read things the way they want to read them, elaborating initial false premises with relish and abandon. They can be glaringly inconsistent in espousing only those facts that suit their purpose, ignoring others that disprove their point. Sophistic paranoid patients find a way to blame others for their errors, weaknesses, and misfortunes, while sophistic psychopaths cleverly cow others to stem criticism.

One patient built a "best defense is a good offense" stratagem around the idea embodied in the proverb, "Let him who is without sin cast the first stone." Knowing that none of us is entirely without sin, he handled all accusers by slapping the label of sinner on them, condemning them in turn on the basis of their minor faults. By staying our hand from casting the first stone, this psychopath dodged the accusation. There was no refutation, only a good trick of logic. (The nonpsychopath might say instead something on the order of, "I'll take criticism only from you whose sins aren't as great as mine.")

These patients confuse sophistic skills with perception. They are proud of their illogical formulations and want us to share in them. They may even embark on a course of proselytizing, promoting ideas that sometimes seem overvalued in inverse proportion to their soundness.

15. Developmental regression. A retreat from maturity is often manifest in interpersonal relationships. All relationships may be transferential, infantile, or absent. An example is narcissistic self-love, in which the relationship with others is turned into a means for serving oneself, or preference for a relationship with the self overrides a need for a relationship with others.

16. Impulsiveness. Feeling and thought are translated directly into behavior, without hand-staying reflection and without regard for consequences. Impulsiveness is found in almost all the disorders, for example, in the schizophrenic responding to delusions, the paranoid unable to control homicidal impulses, the depressed patient unable to control suicidal impulses, and the obsessive-compulsive who interrupts the painful paralysis of brooding by taking impulsive action just to do something.

17. Inefficiency or incompetence. The patient is prone to bumbling or to being openly incompetent. He or she might misfire both socially and at work.

18. Disequilibrium between thought and behavior. It may seem that action replaces thought (impulsivity) or thought replaces action (obsessiveness).

19. Bizarre behavior. The patient captures our attention, or actually startles us, by being weird or strange. Not confined to the peculiar schizophrenic or schizotypal patient, a degree of bizarreness in appearance or behavior is often deliberately or unconsciously cultivated by patients with a neurosis or other personality disorders. An example is the obsessional patient who, afraid that his suit might be ruined by water, carried a large black umbrella on a clear day if the weather report merely mentioned the possibility of rain.

DOING A MENTAL STATUS EVALUATION

A mental status evaluation brings the diagnostic possibilities into focus. In the following section, "The Parameters," broad definitions of the essential mental status parameters are outlined. Suggestions are given for determining mental status (in the section entitled "The Procedure"). And suggestions are given for using mental status material for therapy (in the section entitled "The Therapeutic Implications").

Because changes are often subtle and unexpected, in your evaluation you should go beyond such obvious signs as changes in appearance in schizophrenic, and mood alteration in manic, patients. For example, note such subtle changes of appearance as blandness in the phobic patient and such subtle changes of thought process and content disorder as the above-described self-serving reasoning in the psychopathic/antisocial patient.

The Parameters

The following are the chief mental status parameters along with some of the disorders in which we might expect to find changes.

Appearance

Ask yourself a simple question: What does my patient look like? Be honest. Is he or she beautiful, ugly, weird, ordinary, or "normal." (For present purposes *normal* is broadly used to mean "blending in.")

Well-known examples of changes in appearance are weirdness from the schizotypal spectrum, fussiness and prissiness from the obsessional spectrum, and seductiveness from the hysterical spectrum. Less familiar changes in appearance are plainness of the avoidant patient and conformity in the social phobic.

Example. A borderline patient when "divesting herself of all her objects"—that is, when angry at the world and everyone in it—dressed to resemble a witch. Especially notable were her too-pointed hat and her long black cape.

Example. The abovementioned obsessive patient, who always carried an umbrella on sunny days because "if it rains, it will ruin my custom-made suit," was seen on the street by his therapist, who reported: "It was a beautiful sunny day. Everybody looked happy. Everybody was wearing loose clothing, open at the neck, appearing pretty and cool. They were dressed in pastel whites, yellows, and pinks. And here's this man in the middle of them all: dark black suit, black shoes, long pointy black umbrella. Everyone knew something was wrong with him."

Speech

This is how the patient talks. (The content of speech, what the patient says, is best included under *thought*.) Examples of speech disturbances are echolalia found in schizophrenia, clanging found in manics, overabstract speech and repetitive speech found in obsessionals, and seductive speech found in hysterics and psychopaths.

Example. An obsessive patient believed all his thoughts were stained with sexual and aggressive feelings, of which he was ashamed. As a consequence he rarely, if ever, said what he felt. He became discursive in speech, circumstantial, too refined, and used big words that were beloved because they obscured his meaning rather than conveyed it. Obsessional undoing from guilt was manifest in uncertainty, expressed in and created by his ending each sentence with, "Is that right?"—driving others to distraction.

Though typically shame and embarrassment about problems with speech tempt both the therapist and the patient either to ignore speech difficulties or to give an organic rather than a psychological explanation for those perceived, mannerisms and affectations such as a lisp and changes such as sputtering and stuttering are sometimes caused by emotional problems.

Thought

The disorder may be of what we think (thought content) and/or how we think it (thought process). Examples of thought content disorder are delusions of persecution and hallucinations. Examples of thought process disorder are disorganization of thinking, loosening of associations, and the familiar tangentiality and circumstantiality. The therapist might suspect thought disorder when he or she finds him- or herself disagreeing with the patient because the patient is dereistic; unable to understand the patient because the patient is loose, disorganized, or wanders off the point; annoyed with the patient because the patient is circumstantial, repeating him- or herself over and over without ever getting to the point; or frustrated with the patient because the patient is overinclusive, postponing answering a simple question out of the need to start at the beginning.

Therapists who readily identify thought process and thought content disorder in the psychoses less readily identify them in other mental disorders and in the normal. For example, we rarely identify as thought disorder the hesitant thinking in some fearful phobics or the overelaborations of some theatrical, exaggerating hysterics. Too, we rarely identify normal magical thinking as a thought disorder, wherein superstition reigns and superhuman feats are considered possible. For example, one counterman played a number that came up twice on his cash register, irrationally believing there to be a connection between his cash register and the winning number to come.

Behavior

Behavior is how the patient acts, noted by him- or herself, you, or others. Behavior expresses thought nonverbally. Examples include the following:

1. Masochistic behavior that expresses zero-sum thinking—self-depriving behavior resulting from the belief that there is a finite amount of $\times$ in this world, and if I get some, you lose some.

2. Traumatic behavior. Some nonproductive, maladaptive, or self-destructive behavior is traumatic in origin and repeated in an attempt at mastery.

3. Nontransferential acting out. Here the individual who is not in therapy avoids awareness and understanding of problems via pressured, frantic, and often self-destructive activity. Examples include covering or dissipating depression by overspending, stealing, gambling, or substance abuse (the latter applies when it is used to create a false sense of control and security). For example, one patient stole small things to prove he would never go without essentials, "not if I can help it."

4. Transference behaviors. Examples of transference behaviors that are the product of a specific underlying disorder (discussed in greater detail in chapter 11) include the following:

a. Schizoid isolation from the therapist.

b. Schizotypal attempts to get the therapist to participate in medical craziness.

One patient, incorrectly believing her problems were the product of a yeast infection, demanded antiyeast medication, not psychotherapy.

c. Paranoid suspiciousness. One patient said, "You asked that question, not to get information, but as a ploy to see how I would react."

d. Dependent stagnation. Excessive dependency on the therapist can preclude real-life evolution.

e. Passive-aggressive indirect hostility. We see indirect passive-aggressive assaults on the therapist's feelings, schedule, or finances, or in defeating therapy in order to defeat the therapist.

f. Hypomanic flight into health/depressive self-destructive acting out when expressive of premature, inappropriate optimism or pessimism about treatment.

g. Hysterical seductiveness. Seduction of the therapist may be openly sexual, or symbolically sexual, as for example, in prying into the therapist's private life.

h. Obsessive-compulsive withholding, torturing, submissiveness, control, stubbornness, or disdainful superiority, often moral.

i. Psychopathic misuse of therapy or the therapist. An example is the patient who fakes psychosis so as to be found incompetent to stand trial.

Insight

Insight is the ability to recognize our problems. Insight is less often absent than limited in scope, so that the patient sees some but not all of the problems. It is also often limited in depth, so that the patient knows he or she has a problem but not why (superficial, rather than deep, insight).

Judgment

Judgment is the capacity to identify and implement a course of action that is appropriate, purposeful, constructive, fulfilling, and creative. Shifting and arbitrary social and moral values often make it difficult for the therapist to decide if judgment is good or bad. Sometimes the decision concerning good/bad judgment is (unfairly) made in hindsight—so that if the patient fails, the judgment was bad, and if the patient succeeds, the judgment was good.

Example. The problem of what is good or bad judgment is illustrated by the patient who debated about leaving a dull, ordinary job as a clinic nurse and striking out, at an advanced age, to become a solo nurse practitioner. The patient was aware that she was exchanging certainty for uncertainty, a steady for an unsteady salary, and this for a plan whose success was not by any means assured. Leaving her job in one sense looked reckless (bad judgment) but in another, creative (good judgment).

Memory

Impairment may be functional (as in hysterical amnesia) or organic (as in Alzheimer's disease). Memory impairment may be of recall (immediate), recent memory (a few minutes or longer), or remote memory (distant past).

When you test for memory, always remember this: the inability to remember is often due to anxiety, not memory defect. Anxiety can cause memory deficit in the healthy individual and worsen it in the patient who already has organic memory impairment.

Orientation

Like memory impairment, disorientation may be functional (as in fugues) or organic (as in Alzheimer's disease or coma). Orientation impairment is divided into impairment of orientation to time, place, and person. Impairment of orientation to time may be a true disorientation or the result of memory deficit (you have to remember the time to know what time it is).

The Procedure

Test for mental status parameters appropriately. For example, it may not be necessary to test for memory in the intact, functioning patient.

Test selectively. Emphasize those parts of the exam according to your tentative differential diagnosis.

Test with sensitivity. If you choose to test memory in the intact, functioning patient, ask a question more challenging than "Name the president of the United States." If necessary, be apologetic. You might say, "Can we take a few moments to do some formal testing? I know some of these questions seem very elementary, but humor me; I have to ask them, and, who knows, we might even find something of interest, perhaps surprising."

Use the results wisely. Being off on the date does not mean the patient per se has a memory deficit.

The Therapeutic Implications

Most patients tolerate discussion of their symptoms better than they tolerate a discussion of disordered mental status parameters such as appearance, speech, thought, behavior, and judgment. These are often "me" manifestations, unlike many symptoms, which are often "not me." The patient's self-esteem and pride is easily wounded when we talk about his or her funny outfit or strange speech. We seem to be picking on the patient. In particular, most patients are pleased with their appearance, and even when the patient asks the therapist for suggestions, they are, if given, often resented, with the patient insulted by the suggestion that he or she does not look as good as possible. Since any confrontation, clarification, or interpretation of appearance is easily misunderstood as a criticism, it may be best for the therapist to work on other areas of the patient's problems, hoping that appearance will change as the patient improves in other modalities. The same is true for speech pattern disturbance.

Example. A patient believed he sputtered and stuttered for physiological reasons, but in fact sputtered and stuttered because he was afraid to express himself, because he did not feel entitled to express himself, because speaking meant saying forbidden things, because he wished to tease others by withholding his speech, and because he perceived the act of speaking to be a hostile and so forbidden assault. The therapist reserved the dynamic explanation of the patient's speech problems for a *behavioral* context—his shyness—more acceptable because it elicited less shame. The problems with speech then disappeared in resonance as the parallel problems in behavior were understood, analyzed, and abandoned.

In contrast, patients are usually less defensive about their thought disorder. In fact, the patient discussing his or her thought disorder often feels not put-down but challenged to an intellectual duel. Too, the therapist should promptly identify and challenge disordered thinking. Unlike disordered appearance and most disordered speech, disordered thinking interferes with the therapeutic interaction. For example, the illogical paranoid who blames everyone else, including the therapist, for his or her fate should from the start be requested to take some responsibility for his or her own actions. He or she should be firmly asked, or directed, to stop distorting perceptions of him- or herself and of the real world so that he or she can create a blameless image of him- or herself and an adversary or persecutor of others. If this is not done, the patient will soon see the therapist as the cause of, not the cure for, all his or her problems and will fail to form a healthy therapeutic alliance. Similarly requiring prompt identification and treatment are the illogic of the schizotypal patient whose motto is "the queerer the better," the hypomanic who believes every minor triumph is an occasion for a major celebration, the obsessive-compulsive who believes that everything is worth considering and so fails to make priority lists, and the psychopath who tells him- or herself and his or her therapist lies in order to gain a temporary advantage in the real world.

The therapist can more easily discourage pathological thinking when he or she maintains the separation of thought from feeling—a separation that is pathological in real life but suitable for therapeutic purposes. Like the obsessional who maintains isolation of affect from thought so that he or she may continue to think hostile or sexual thoughts (acceptable as long as they are intellectual, unemotional preoccupations), the therapist maintains the same isolation, but so that he or she can better think the patient's problems through with the patient. Thus to the sensitive patient the formulation "You *think* angry thoughts about me?" can be more palatable and so more therapeutic than "You *feel* angry with me?" And "You are *thinking* about suicide?" is more palatable and thus more therapeutic than "You are *feeling* suicidal?"

Disordered judgment may have serious consequences requiring a multipronged attack, perhaps heroic. This might consist of such supportive (noninsight-creating) techniques as advice, sharing experiences, interdiction, giving permission, encouraging identification, and ego lending, as well as insight-creating clarification and interpretation. Hospitalization may be required to interrupt a self-generating process, evaluate the patient medically, begin medication, and/ or prevent suicidal or homicidal behavior.

REFERENCE

Kantor, Martin. *Determining Mental Status*. Springfield, Ill.: Charles C. Thomas, 1988.

Chapter 5

Goals and Objectives

Goals and objectives (Dr. Henry Pinsker [1988] suggests that a goal is a therapist's expectation, while an objective is a patient's expectation) are difficult to formulate because treatment is an art as well as a science, and patients are complex and unpredictable. As a result many therapists proceed with but an impressionistic idea of what is wrong and what needs to be changed. Their answer to the question, Where are we going? is in many cases an unsatisfactory, though heartfelt, Forward, I hope.

CHARACTERISTIC DEFECTS OF TREATMENT GOALS

The following are some characteristic defects of treatment goals:

1. Impressionistic. The therapist might sense the patient needs insight but fail to specify insight into what. Or the therapist might suggest that interpersonal relationships need to be improved and the ego strengthened. But both interpersonal relationships and egos have a number of components, some of which probably do and some of which probably do not need improvement and strengthening.

2. Inspirational. The therapist, sensing that having insight is good, recommends that the patient have more.

3. Unreachable. Marriage is not possible (or desirable) for everyone. Not all

patients can make their unconscious conscious. Many obsessionals will remain ritualistic; many hysterics will continue to somatize; and so on.

4. Trivial. One therapist was inordinately proud of having removed a phobia of mice in a schizophrenic patient who continued to be delusional.

5. Rote. Do not take goals from a list then use them unmodified for your patient.

6. Inflexible. Goals change with treatment. Achieving one goal changes the others. For example, a schizophrenic who at the beginning has a delusional (grandiose) goal of improving interpersonal relationships may abandon it following pharmacotherapy for his or her delusions, or may abandon it in favor of internal peace once the capacity for self-assessment, another goal, is attained.

Too many therapists are terrified at the prospect of formulating a treatment plan. They are not only terrified, they also bristle because they feel controlled by powerful, unseen, potentially assaultive enemy forces (e.g., the utilization review committee).

BASIC QUESTIONS TO ASK YOURSELF

The task is easier, and goals will appear more obvious, if the therapist asks him- or herself the following questions:

1. What is wrong with this patient? Patients may have signs and symptoms, of an Axis I disorder (an obsession, for example) or from Axis II (a personality disorder). They may also have interpersonal difficulties, behavioral problems, existential problems, and realistic problems (either self-induced or the result of bad luck).

2. Does the patient need treatment? Some people do not. That the patient needs treatment is too often assumed and not always specifically stated.

3. What is and what is not to be treated? Though it sounds like a good thing to do, treating the whole patient is usually impractical, often impossible.

4. Are we to palliate or cure? Are symptoms to be removed or merely reduced in breadth and/or intensity? The following are examples of palliation:

An obsessive-compulsive patient learned to substitute neutral philosophical ruminations for ruminations that were frightening because deemed obscene. A phobic patient learned to substitute a fear of subways, which he could avoid by walking to work, for a fear of elevators, which he had to take to reach his office on the high floor of a high-rise building.

5. What are to be our methods of treatment? The therapist does not have to think this through on his or her own. Many volumes have been written on ways to treat. The therapist who quotes others rather than reinventing the wheel courts glory, not shame.

Examples of methods of treatment follow:

Developing Insight

The therapist first notes who needs the insight. Patients may complain about their problems, have problems that are only the object of complaints of others, or have problems heretofore unnoticed by either the patient or family.

Second, there should be a statement about insight into what. An example comes from a short-term therapy case treated and presented by Dr. Elizabeth Zetzel involving a young man afraid to drive over a bridge to meet the girl he was to marry. He was afraid the car would get out of control, and he would be injured. Relief followed insight into the origin of the symptom in unresolved Oedipus.

Then the therapist notes what is expected from the insight. Will the patient have symptomatic, behavioral, or existential improvement, or all three.

Finally, the therapist speculates on how insight is expected to produce change. The therapist might say, "This patient will improve when he learns how infantile his excessive perfectionism is."

Replacing Fantasy with Reality (Reality Testing)

The therapist might identify the patient's reality, then the therapist's reality, and contrast the two. Thus a patient who feared his aged mother would go to live with his sister and be convinced by the sister to change her will, cutting him out of his inheritance, was reminded that, in the therapist's opinion, this was unlikely to happen because the mother loved him, could not stand the sister, and the sister could not stand the mother.

Reassessing a Distorted Self-Image

The therapist and the patient test reality in this special area. The patient's actual self is contrasted with the fantasied self. Schizophrenics may have to reassess their conviction that the self is mutilated, depressed patients that the self is defective, narcissistic and grandiose patients that the self is perfect, anorexic patients that the self is too fat, or obese patients that the self is too thin.

Replacing Id with Ego

Here the patient's instincts are softened, covered, or buried. There are several ways to soften, cover, or bury the instincts. For example, one can do it verbally (exhortation—e.g., "Calm down!"), cognitively (teaching the patient to avoid self-arousal), or with psychotropic medication. This fosters ego-healing, strengthening, and development.

Changing the Defensive Structure

(This is also discussed in chapter 9.) This can be done in one of several ways:

A defense can be altered behaviorally. The patient may be asked to face the anxiety behind the defense. The above-mentioned obsessional patient who carried an umbrella on clear days lest it begin to rain on and ruin his suit was asked to go out of the house on cloudy days without an umbrella, and to think about how his suit, if it got wet, could be rescued by a simple, inexpensive cleaning, and how if worse came to worse, he could throw it away and buy another.

A defense can be modified consciously. Examples include strengthening repression (e.g., by telling the patient to forget about this, overlook that); supporting undoing over doing (e.g., suggesting atonement); or creating identification with a benign therapist to replace identification with a malignant mother.

A defense can be substituted. A healthy defense is substituted for one less healthy. This is often done by education. The defenses of sublimation, repression, and reaction formation can be recommended as being generally healthy. Sublimation might be substituted for regression, repression for denial, and reaction formation for projection.

A defense may be analyzed. Here its origin is uncovered with clues obtained from the transference. Thus the obsessional who must have everything perfectly neat needs to know how her neatness is meaningful—for example, in being a solution, if substitutive, to feeling defective. We might trace the origins of this feeling defective to inappropriate behavior on the part of the parents who were misguided in their treatment of the patient as defective, only doing so because of problems of their own. The therapist can illustrate his or her point using the patient's behavior in the session: for example, how the patient fusses with her clothing when she feels criticized by the therapist.

Softening the Superego

Describe the nature of the patient's conscience: "You are a moral person!— but in some ways too moral!" Then advise the patient that his or her superego is too punitive, too permissive, too unpredictably permissive first then punitive next, and so on. Since the superego was formed through early identification, it can be reformed through later identification (with the therapist).

Replacing Determinism with Free Will

Patients often believe compulsive attitudes and behaviors represent preferences. In one case a patient was helped to see how what he believed was a freely chosen dislike of competition was actually a compulsion to avoid its feared consequences.

Replacing Defective and Unrewarding Personal and Professional Interpersonal Relationships with Effective, Rewarding Ones

Often accomplished through exhortation, advice, training, and behavioral techniques, this improves the patient's lot at home with his family, and outside at work and with friends. Not only is the origin and development of the interpersonal problem studied, but also bad and good companions are identified and new choices recommended. Symptomatic improvement often follows interpersonal improvement. For example, one depressed patient who turned good friends into enemies was told to stop backbiting; he found himself better loved and thus less depressed. Another patient treated for his tendency to pick psychopathic women because they were "refreshingly different from my overly controlling, obsessive mother" not only married a solid citizen but lost a phobia of being driven over a high bridge.

6. What cannot be done? This should include both the unlikely and the impossible. Humane and medicolegal considerations dictate that the therapist not make promises he or she cannot keep, either because the state of the art is inadequate or because the patient will live out negative feelings about therapy by failure to make progress just to defeat what may be the perfect therapist and therapy. It is better that the overly pessimistic therapist be prepared to become overly optimistic instead of the other way around. The patient will be disappointed to learn that changes will be limited; but since most of us like ourselves as we are, the patient will also find it reassuring that he or she will emerge, not as a new person, but as a more satisfactory version of the old. Many patients who say they want complete change in fact find this frightening. Many patients are like the patient with an impulse disorder who, bothered not by the impulsiveness, but by the resultant guilt and social problems, would secretly have liked to have kept his problems if only he could have avoided the consequences.

An unavoidable danger is that some patients use awareness of the limitations of therapy as a resistance to continuing treatment. Thus one geriatric patient insisted, "I'm too old to change completely," doing so primarily to avoid any change at all.

7. Are there any complications of achieving one's goals? Help often comes with unpleasant side effects. Thus the passive dependent patient who matures and becomes independent may temporarily (or permanently) feel anxious, the borderline who forms a lasting relationship may feel overwhelmed or devoured—experiencing loss of identity—and the obsessive who takes our good advice may feel controlled and pushed around.

8. How long will it take? Discuss the time frame. The patient needs to know that therapy is sometimes a slow, exacting process, not a miracle cure. The patient should be told, "Since you didn't develop your problems overnight, they will not get better overnight." The formal working-through period—after the patient has learned about him- or herself and now must put the learning to use—

is typically agonizingly slow (and difficult to justify to utilization review). Of course, remember that you, the therapist, often have more time (this is your job) than the patient (this is his or her life), and move as quickly as possible.

9. What does the patient want for him- or herself? Respect self-fulfillment, autonomy, and self-assertiveness. Help the patient formulate goals based on what he or she wants, not on what you want. Your good ideas should supplement but not supplant the patient's. Patients never fail to surprise us. One hospitalized patient was referred to a sheltered workshop; instead she signed out against advice, joined the circus, and became a starring trapeze artist.

Especially to be avoided is the tendency to minister based on one's current interests, or one's current problems. For example, one therapist overly enmeshed in problems of dependency of her own treated all her patients as if they too were overly dependent.

IN CONCLUSION

Also keep in mind the following:

1. Flexibility. Treatment plans should not be etched in stone but should be revised periodically as circumstances warrant.

2. Creativeness. The creative and the inspirational should find room in every treatment plan. After the first, often urgent goals are achieved—for example, symptom removal, reduction of anxiety, and improvement of the patient's activities of daily living—what often remains are such vague, difficult-to-formulate, goals as elusive as personality revision or the goal of self-actualization. (This is to be distinguished from how, the longer the therapy, the more elusive the goal becomes as involvement in the work of therapy obscures its direction.)

The therapist should not assume elusive goals to be unimportant goals. And he or she must stand firm as to the importance of the quality-of-life goals, even though these are vague, because their nature is hard to adequately define and document, and time-consuming and expensive to achieve. (Indeed, it is often not as expensive as first believed. Therapy once a week for a year at an average of $80 a session costs about $4,000, less than many surgical procedures.) In one case it took the therapist 25 years to work through the problems that kept a young patient isolated from men, eventually enabling her, at age 45, to get a steady male friend, if not to marry—a goal worthy and rewarding, though time-consuming and expensive. (Throughout the utilization review, the committee implied there was self-serving therapist behavior, the fostering of pathological dependency in the patient, and other dastardly deeds such as the incompetence of using "outdated psychotherapy" in place of "modern pharmacological treatment.")

3. Honesty. When there is insurance and long-term treatment has to be justified to utilization review, inventions abound that introduce parameters to treatment. One therapist treating a patient who had coverage only for crisis intervention created a cycling affective disorder even though the patient was chronically

depressed. He did this so that each and every report to the utilization review could describe a fresh, newly emergent, mood swing. Now, the illness was not chronic but had a beginning and end, and was expected to respond to a discrete, codifiable, quantifiable therapeutic intervention. Another therapist justified his patient's lack of progress over the years by saying, "He needs treatment, if not to get better then to keep him from getting worse." The patient who sees the insurance form is aware of duplicity and may feel used or may believe the therapist to be dishonest. Worse, he or she may even come to believe the content of the dishonesty—because "my therapist would not say it in writing if it were not at least partly true."

4. Efficiency. This is not to say that some therapists do not proceed too slowly, do not try to do too much, or see the patient as an annuity. Some postpone achievement of goals so that the therapist and the patient can "continue the process of revision of the underlying personality disorder"—really with nothing better in mind than a kind of exorcism of pathology or "attainment of genitality." A weak excuse may be given to the patient for prolonging treatment, for example, by giving unrealistic or unacceptable goals artificial legitimacy, or peripheral goals artificial importance. A patient, advised to do so by her therapist, postponed her marriage so that she could "enter the marriage free of problems that were likely to appear and then interfere with it." (Anticipating trouble before it starts may be academically valid but is rarely practical and, since most of us are unpredictable, may represent less a form of treatment than a form of excessive caution.)

5. Modesty. Much improvement is fortuitous improvement. The disorder is self-limited, the precipitant disappears, or simple "tincture of time" suffices to heal.

Even when therapy is sought for and directed to specific matters, such as sexual problems or marriage difficulties, other contiguous areas of the patient's life may be improved not directly but coincidentally.

REFERENCE

Pinsker, Henry. Supportive Therapy. A paper based on Grand Rounds presentations at Beth Israel and at St. Vincent's Hospital, New York City, in January 1988.

Chapter 6

Modes of Treatment

INTRODUCTION

How do we determine what treatment is best for an individual patient?

Rarely is there only one way to treat the patient with an emotional disorder. Sometimes there is a preferred treatment, be it pharmacotherapy for acute mania, behavioral therapy and pharmacotherapy for phobia, or interpersonal therapy and pharmacotherapy for schizophrenia. Usually a variety of therapeutic approaches will work, either because a given problem has a number of satisfactory solutions or because therapies are more alike than unalike.

In this chapter in section one, we discuss the helpful elements from all rational psychotherapies. For example, all rational psychotherapies offer the patient the willingness to listen, interest, noncritical acceptance, and a plan, explicit or implicit, for change. In section two, we describe some advantages and disadvantages of the more familiar psychotherapies.

The therapist is advised to select not only the best approach for the patient but also the approach with which he or she is most comfortable, and which is most suitable for his or her personality/personality problems. When two or more possibilities suggest themselves, the therapist should either select the one with the most advantages and the fewest disadvantages, or combine them (e.g., insight and behavioral approaches).

HELPFUL ELEMENTS FROM ALL RATIONAL
PSYCHOTHERAPIES

Here are some of the many ways all rational psychotherapists and psychotherapies influence, for the better, the way people think, feel, and behave.

1. Encouragement. All (except sadistic) therapists, whether analytically,
cognitively, behaviorally, or biologically oriented, encourage improvement by
conveying the wish, spoken or unspoken, to see improvement.

2. Welcome. All therapists, by agreeing to see the patient for help, extend
a welcoming hand to the patient. They are like the club that accepts or the
employer who hires.

3. Hope. The mere act of accepting a patient into treatment gives him or
her hope that better days are ahead.

4. Information. All good therapists knowingly or unwittingly follow Jerome
Weinberger's definition of *psychotherapy* as a process of telling the patient what
he or she needs to know in order to survive and prosper (personal communication). This information, when not the *point* of the therapist's remarks, may
be slyly given *in passing*, gleaned by the patient from what is purportedly
intended otherwise, for example, what is intended to be a clarification or interpretation (defined elsewhere.)

5. Permission. As with information, the therapist may either give permission
directly or through clarifications, interpretations, and so on, given in such a way
that they will be heard as intended permission.

Example. A patient hesitated to buy a sports car because he was afraid he was not
behaving maturely but in a "phallic narcissistic fashion." Intended permission to buy
the car was given, not directly, but in the guise of a clarificatory question: "You believe
the car is just a phallus?" By this question the therapist clarified the patient's unconscious
equation, car = phallus, while also implying, It is not just a phallus, it is also a car;
you are not a phallic narcissist just because you want and need a sports car; so go ahead.

6. Absolution. The therapist recognizes excessive guilt and forgives.

7. Reassurance. Therapist neutrality is a form of calm that by itself diminishes patient anxiety. One patient, hard-pressed to afford it, bought a second
home before selling the first. He felt extremely anxious until he realized his
therapist did not seem to think he had ruined himself. He said, "Things must
not be so bad, Doc, if you aren't upset about what I've done."

8. Organization. Even an incorrect or harmful formulation when repeated
with regularity can have an organizing, and so calming effect.

9. Regularity. Regularity of sessions, over and above their content, can have
an organizing, and so calming, effect.

10. Predictability. Predictable responses, over and above their content, can
have an organizing, and so calming, effect.

11. Positive response. The patient feels liked, not hated; accepted, not cast

out; respected, not demeaned; praised, not criticized. Patients who believe that if others find them defective, then it must be so, are especially responsive.

12. Positive relationship. This refers to real aspects of the relationship (still within professional, not personal, bounds). The therapist might provide direct gratification by saying, "I'm glad you seem less anxious," or by feeding the patient symbolically, with a cough drop, or a cup of coffee. This gives the patient an immediate lift and promises better things to come. It reminds the patient that there are nice people in the world to meet. (Of course, this is a dangerous technique when used with patients who will suspect our motives—i.e., with patients who are paranoid. And it is a dangerous technique with all patients when overused.)

13. Undoing of the poisonous past. Patients come to us tortured by what Dr. Sheila Hafter Gray liked to call poisonous introjects. Poisonous introjects are malignant people from our past who have been incorporated into our psyche and who are now carried around with us like a heavy, prickly load. They purposely stir up forbidden instincts, and tell us we are defective or worthless. Present company who produce a negative—for example, devaluing—effect often do so by reawakening sleeping poisonous introjects. Most patients after hearing from poisonous introjects will seek another opinion. But too often the patient gets this "second opinion" from friends and family who are also malignant or who, if benign, do not have behind them the weight of authority to make the different opinion stick. In contrast, a therapist is benign. By *benign* is meant that he or she behaves in a way different from the patient's poisonous parents or malignant past society, or if behaving in the same way, does it for a different, kinder reason. And a therapist has the weight of authority.

14. Empathy. This tells the patient, I understand.

15. Manipulation. We refer of course to manipulation for the good of the patient. In manipulation the therapist produces a desired effect insidiously. Implicit suggestion—such as by asking leading questions—sly allusion or implication, and calculated nonverbal communication are examples. An example of manipulation by asking leading questions is the question asked by the oncologist who suspected his patient's excessive vomiting after chemotherapy had hysterical overlay: "Do you have an oversensitive stomach?" An example of manipulation by allusion or implication is used by the psychopharmacologist who manipulates the patient psychologically with the placebo effect. And an example of manipulation by nonverbal communication is raising one's eyebrows.

16. Transference management. (This is discussed in detail in chapter 11.) Effective therapies successfully analyze, manipulate, or bypass transference. By *transference* is meant the patient's tendency to repeat, with every new acquaintance, the essential facts of his or her emotional disorder. Freud analyzed transference, Jay Haley manipulated it (e.g., in his use of reverse psychology), and other therapists bypass it. Attempting to bypass interfering transference—both negative, such as stubbornness, and positive, such as erotic—are the cognitive therapist trying to have a discussion of maladaptive thinking and the behaviorist trying to condition or recondition.

Example. A psychopharmacologist had a patient who refused to take his medication because he believed himself ordered about now as he was ordered about when he was a child. The doctor responded, not by ordering the patient about once again, but by educating the patient to the need to take the medication, pointing out such things as the advantages and disadvantages. In this way he bypassed mindless rebellion appropriate for then, not now. This interaction by extension resolved other mindless rebellions, contributory to the present illness. The patient had not only a helpful pharmacological but also a helpful psychotherapeutic effect.

ADVANTAGES AND DISADVANTAGES OF DIFFERENT MODES OF TREATMENT

The following are some of the more commonly used modes of treatment, each with some of its advantages and disadvantages. (Insight therapy is discussed further in Chapter 8.)

Pharmacotherapy

Introduction

Some condemn pharmacotherapy as mind and behavior control. But such control is not always a bad thing. As an example we take the patient in her late 80s who screams at night, waking the neighbors, who can either be maintained at home on medication or have to enter a nursing home. In the nursing home we see patients who have an organically caused emotional disorder disrupt other patients. We may have a choice between keeping these patients in the nursing home on medication or removing them from the nursing home by transferring them to a psychiatric hospital.

Advantages

Psychotropic medication, correctly selected and correctly prescribed, can accomplish the following:

1. Treatment of anxiety and of symptoms employed to master anxiety, such as obsessions.

2. Treatment of the pathological mood, both depression and hypomania/mania. This includes depressive equivalents such as headaches and other depressive manifestations such as some agoraphobia.

3. Treatment of functional and organic psychotic symptoms. For example, disorganized thought may be slowed directly (medication effect) or indirectly (thinking becomes organized when disorganizing anger is reduced).

4. Treatment of maladaptive or disruptive behavior, such as some antisocial, angry, impulsive, homicidal, suicidal or otherwise self-destructive behavior (e.g., factitious disorder).

5. Treatment of selected undesirable/maladaptive personality traits and dis-

order. This involves (a) antipsychotic medication when characterological behavior is the product of micropsychotic episodes (some paranoid and some borderline behavior); (b) antidepressants or antimanic agents such as lithium when characterological behavior is the product of mood swings (some argumentativeness, overzealousness); (c) anxiolytics when characterological behavior is an expression of anxiety (some avoidant behavior).

Of course, if the therapist is not a physician, or if a physician-therapist prefers not to do the prescribing, believing it, for example, to contaminate the transference, an appropriate referral can and should be made.

Disadvantages

1. Deflects from the education/learning approach to a resolution of problems.

2. May give a false sense of well-being, thereby reducing the motivation to correct intrapsychic and extrapsychic problems.

3. May make the patient too detached or "spacey" to function at work or in relationships.

4. May have other unpleasant side effects. Examples include loss of interest that can be confused with schizophrenic anhedonia or depression; dizziness; and interference with sexual desire or performance.

5. May have physically dangerous side effects, for example, a fall in blood pressure or tardive dyskinesia.

6. May be addicting, especially when misused with alcohol and in combination with other drugs—in particular by passive dependent patients and psychopathic/antisocial patients. (This is especially true for the benzodiazepines and some antidepressants. In this regard caution is advised with any patient who has a self-diagnosis of panic attacks and a self-prescribed course of benzodiazepines.)

7. May be used for inappropriate reasons. Drugs should be used to reduce target psychopathology, not for control, and not for punishment when the patient is unpalatable, boring, or threatens the therapist by making him or her anxious.

8. May cease to work after having been effective for one or more episodes of illness. A possible example is that of the patient with a unipolar depression, occurring about every six years, who responded several times to antidepressants alone but eventually had to have psychotherapy to supplement pharmacotherapy.

Group Therapy

Advantages

1. Can be used to treat many patients at once.

2. Can harness the expertise of other members of the group. They can contribute to the patient's treatment from their own experience and outside individual therapy.

3. Can be especially effective for the patient who listens to peers more than to authority.

4. Can handle subjects that individual treatment tends to avoid. Included here are topics considered by some individual therapists to be not momentous enough for individual therapy (some personal existential problems and timely but evanescent topics).

5. Can provide the patient with an enjoyable experience and so is recreational as well as therapeutic.

6. Can be a temporary substitute for real relationships, for example, a transitional peer group. This can be especially helpful for isolated schizoid and lonely, depressed patients.

Disadvantages

1. Intrapsychic problems are often obscured by focus on the group process and/or group problems.

2. The individual can become lost in the crowd.

3. Intervention by other patients, with problems of their own, can create, not health, but the same problems in others—an example of the blind leading the blind.

4. The patient in both group and individual treatment can play one against the other, for example, using the group's opinions in the service of resistance to individual therapy, or vice versa.

5. Not all therapists like or are suitable for doing group psychotherapy. The more paranoid therapist believes him- or herself observed (even stared at); the more obsessional therapist cannot keep all the crosscurrents straight and becomes confused; and the more depressed therapist, if ganged up on by the group, may become upset and have a fall in self-esteem.

6. Some therapists find the level of discussion boring and the selection of topics uninteresting.

Individual Therapy

Advantages

1. The patient is the center of attention.

2. Only transference/countertransference and sometimes reality intrude, not other patients or drug effects.

3. The patient is given the opportunity to express him- or herself as the therapist listens to the patient and encourages the patient to tell the therapist more. This is in contrast to some other forms of treatment where the therapist, busy "doing to" the patient—by telling the patient of his or her preconceived theories or "inflicting" on the patient his or her treatments—is too preoccupied, too impatient, or too active to listen, and encourages the patient to tell, not more, but less.

4. The transference "illness" can form. This illness does not form, or forms incompletely, in other types of therapy. This illness can, if one likes, be the center of interpretive attention, the grist for the therapeutic mill. Even when not

interpreted (when for the therapist's, not the patient's, ears) transference illness is instructive. For example, it helps the therapist arrive at a thoughtful, precise, in-depth, and complete diagnosis.

5. Since therapy takes place over time, there is an opportunity for revision of errors. The therapist may gradually alter his or her formulation, saying, "Originally I thought . . . but now that we have learned more, I believe . . . "

6. A special, close relationship (professional, not personal) develops between therapist and patient.

Disadvantages

1. It is often lengthy, time-consuming, and expensive.

2. It is a hothouse form of treatment that magnifies both tactical and interpersonal (transference/countertransference) errors. When things go wrong, they can go very wrong and can escalate. Minor mistakes become major errors. There is no counterbalance, as in group therapy, where the other patients can come to the rescue.

3. Because two people work together in self-imposed isolation, therapist attributes assume extraordinary significance. The therapist who is idiosyncratic (e.g., quirky), mean spirited, and so on, can be quite a bad influence.

Insight Therapy (Often Individual)

Advantages

It is a fact that insight produces change. It is a fact that most of us think we know *how* insight produces change. It is also a fact that most of us do not really know all the ways insight works. The land between insight and change is an unknown territory. The mechanisms we cite to explain the change tend to have a concrete, superficial quality to them. Yes, exposing things to light, such as unconscious wishes, allows us to reconsider and reintegrate them. But exactly how does it make a symptom go away?

A patient, a psychotherapist, was unaccountably depressed around Easter. Through self-analysis he clarified that he was depressed because a family canceled a session with him just before the holiday. He realized, "This reminds me of when I was left out of holidays because my parents didn't celebrate them." After understanding the reason, his depression lifted. But he could not put his finger on the *mechanism* by which "I understand" became "I no longer feel depressed."

Some supposed effects of insight are not due to the insight at all. Sometimes they are due to therapist suggestion or appeal to the patient's better judgment. For example, the therapist who says, "Insight is needed here," is also implying, This is a symptom bad to have, I exhort you to give this symptom up, and, You will please me if you do.

Then there is the question of insight into what. The term too often is equated with making the unconscious conscious. But it also refers to making the preconscious conscious, and making new connections between heretofore unconnected conscious matters—present or past.

A fascinating topic (beyond the scope of this text) might be to explore which kinds of insight would be most helpful for which problems. For example, it is often said regarding therapy of the schizophrenic patient, Avoid insight. But this certainly means, Avoid making the unconscious conscious. It probably does not mean, Avoid making connections between heretofore seemingly disparate bits of conscious information. The schizophrenic patient, for example, may very well need to know that he treats his hospital nurse like his mother, even though she is not.

Disadvantages

1. When premature or unpalatable, insight creates anxiety. Regressive or dereistic defenses (regression, projection, denial) may be employed to handle overwhelming anxiety.

2. Most insight is unavoidably critical, so it has the potential to worsen depression.

3. Finally, we fan the flames of strong, barely tolerable transference feelings simply by examining them.

Cognitive Therapy

Advantages

The main advantage is direct, efficient repair of thought disorder, both content and process. Because depression is an illness often effectively treatable with cognitive therapy, we will illustrate some aspects of cognitive therapy using as an example some aspects of depression:

a. Primarily a thought process disorder, with ambivalence a hallmark. It is characteristic of depressive disorder that opposite thoughts coexist. Patients may be dependent (needing love) and independent (wanting to be alone); hostile (hating the world) and loving (unable to do enough for others); in love with themselves and full of hate for themselves. Some examples: A depressed patient felt guilty for the way he neglected his parents and at the same time resentful of them for what he believed was the sadistic way in which they had treated him. A doctor admits that he sometimes feels that his fees deprive the poor of money they need and at other times is equally convinced that his poor patients, simply by being poor, deprive him of the money *he* needs.

An expression of this depressive ambivalence may be the rapid alternation between such depressive symptoms as insomnia and oversleeping and anorexia and overeating, even the mood swings between hypomania and depression.

Ambivalence is also apparent in the attitude of depressive patients toward their depression. Even those who recognize their depression as an affliction and express the strongest desire to be rid of it demonstrate on another level a persistent attachment to their condition.

Cognitive treatment might consist of helping the patient fuse the opposites of black and white into the composite, gray. For example, the therapist might offer, "Think of most people not as all good or all bad but as human, with positive and negative, appealing and unappealing, qualities."

b. Primarily a thought content disorder, with value distortion a hallmark.

(1) Symbolization. Depressive patients tend to attach symbolic importance to events or circumstances that others view as merely a part of life's give and take. Thus a damaged possession may symbolize mortality, for example, the transience of all things, or human perfidy, the carelessness of whoever did the damage. This attitude has affinities with both the obsessional disorder and paranoia: the obsessional patient treating a dent in a chair as if it constituted a catastrophe, and the paranoid patient seeing a threat of assault in an innocent gesture or intonation.

Example. A depressed patient drilled a hole in his kitchen wall so that his stereo wires could go from the living room, through the kitchen, and into the bedroom. Then he began to worry that gas from the kitchen would get into the bedroom. He also experienced an admittedly unreasonable fear that the wall could never be made whole again. He called in an engineer who assured him that his fears were groundless. Nevertheless, the patient went ahead and repaired the hole at some trouble and expense because, he claimed, the small hole "devalued" (figuratively) his dwelling. The mortality symbolism is apparent here not only in the patient's concern over the integrity of his property but also, more directly, in his concern for his own safety.

Excessive symbolization can lead to distortion in comparative values because it is applied with no logical consistency. The significance attached to the loss of a household article, for example, might be equal or greater than the significance attached to missing a crucial appointment, the result of a postponable hunt for the article. Here, too, the parallel with the obsessional disorder is apparent—in the typically obsessional way of failing to distinguish mountains from molehills and so putting everything on the same level.

Cognitive treatment might consist of helping the patient to replace symbolic with realistic interpretation.

(2) Defective inference. Depressive patients tend to draw excessive or unwarranted inferences from specific facts or events. Closely associated with this distortion is making a part into a whole. Thus patients justify their pessimistic view of themselves by generalizing from the aspects of themselves they do not admire and suppressing the significance of more favorable aspects. They follow the same illogic in consciously formulating their view of the world. The partial picture becomes the whole picture; the baneful side of life becomes the essence of life. The effects of this distorted reasoning may be reflected in interpretations

of particular events. It is a factor in the typically depressive tendency to respond excessively to annoyances or reverses.

Example. A patient met a man for the first time. The man made a date with her, but subsequently canceled summarily, saying, "I will call you in a few days." The patient became depressed because her immediate reaction was to assume that the man would not call or that he would make a date then call to cancel again, and that she could expect this treatment from all men.

Sometimes the negative overinferences are highly personal, as with the patient who always assumes that overdue bills, churned out by computers, reflect the exasperation and ill will toward him of particular persons within the billing companies.

Cognitive treatment might consist of helping the patient distinguish the part from the whole, thereby avoiding an overreaction.

(3) Depressive outlook. Depressives view the world as a closed system in which satisfactions are neutralized by the prices that must be paid. The fact that some (though by no means most) human interactions involve zero-sum trade-offs—wherein one party's gain is another's loss—too profoundly influences the thinking and actions of many depressive patients.

Treatment consists of helping the patient to see that, at least for his or her purposes, there is an infinite amount of food, love, money, and so on, in the world.

(4) Depressive existential dilemmas. Common among depressive patients is an obsessive preoccupation with abstract problems. Typically, the problems involve the application of ethical or moral principles to the practical concerns of life. An example: How can one live in a society that tolerates practices and conditions at variance with its professed ideals? These questions are often valid in a social or philosophical context, but often have little relevance to the patient's needs or problems. Rather, they are more like screens or surrogates for other unresolved problems that lie at the root of the depressive disorder. Thus one patient who agonized over the inability of society to combine equitable distribution with free-market incentives (communist-capitalistic brooding) was unknowingly reliving a zero-sum conflict between his developing sexual needs and the demands of his repressive parents.

For the luxury of ruminating on these eschatological questions, patients pay a high price. Intensive rumination detracts from concentration on exterior matters. As a result patients tend to achieve below their potential. In addition, they are less likely to become involved in activities from which they might derive normal pleasure. (Some rumination, even with typical depressive subject matter, is not necessarily abnormal. Normal persons, however, control the activity, rather than the other way around. Their ruminations are broken off more frequently and for longer periods than those of depressive patients. Also, they tend to be less intense and more diverse in content.)

Why do patients let this happen to them? A principal reason is escape into fantasy; the obsessional ruminating, however painful, represents escape from a reality that offers patients even greater pain, the pain of confrontation with situations with which they are unable to cope. Another reason is a misplaced ego ideal; patients believe their brooding to be a worthy pursuit, not for everybody, but for the intellectual elite they see themselves belonging to. In essence they say to themselves, Only a smart person like me would realize the universal importance of these matters. Finally, there is masochism, the pain-pleasure of unremitting self-flagellation.

Cognitive treatment might consist of showing the patient the ways the patient works him or herself into depression.

Disadvantages

Presumes rationality and unemotionalism in patients often irrational and emotional.

Behavioral Therapy (Often Individual)

The therapist alters manifest behavior through such techniques as biofeedback, teaching self-control, corrective emotional experience, retraining, and reconditioning. (Details are beyond the scope of this text.) Because the emphasis is on the manifest behavior, not its developmental or dynamic origins, behavioral approaches modify the symptom without necessarily modifying underlying fantasy. For example, one bridge phobic learned to drive over bridges while not unlearning his fear of castration. (This does not mean that symptom substitution, discussed below, invariably occurs.) Relationships with others improve when the symptomatic behavior has disrupted supportive, or created adversarial, interpersonal relationships.

Analytic approaches may be supplemented with a behavioral approach, sometimes called a parameter. In the behavioral parameter used to supplement the analytic treatment of phobics, the phobic patient is asked to face his or her trivial prompt directly. While the behaviorist does this to make it possible to next *decondition* the phobia (perhaps in situ), the analyst instead does this so that aroused fantasy can be used to better understand and analyze the phobia.

Similarly, the patient being analyzed for a post-traumatic stress disorder may be asked to try to revive an encounter with his or her original trauma, for example, by returning to the place where it occurred.

Advantages

Efficient, rapid symptom removal for selected patients.

Disadvantages

1. Often directed to a patient's chief complaint. The complaint (especially in patients with limited insight) may differ from the patient's present illness. Thus

one patient with the principal complaint of phobia of germs had in fact the present illness of obsessive-compulsive fear of dirt.

2. Beneficial effects may be due to spontaneous remission (typical for patients such as borderlines and schizophrenics, also prone to spontaneous relapse), or symptom abandonment followed by symptom substitution, especially in patients who are able to express their pathology in a number of ways. For example, in one patient a depressive headache could substitute effectively for an obsessive worry.

While some believe the fear of substitution is overdone, others believe substitution is *more* of a problem than heretofore believed, because substitution often goes unnoticed. For example, the therapist who expects symptom substitution may look only for a substitutive neurotic or psychotic symptom, but not for a substitute characterological symptom. (Even when looked for, the characterological symptom may be too subtle to be noticed.)

Supportive Therapy

Some things therapists mean by *supporting* are these:

1. Producing a sense of well-being, contrasted with producing a feeling of dysphoria.

2. Providing a crutch, with drugs; inspiration ("you can do it even at your age"); environmental manipulation; and so on.

3. Covering rather than uncovering (expressing). In this sense ECT is supportive, psychoanalysis is not.

4. Symbolically replacing something missing, often love.

5. Doing no harm.

We may not know if we have or have not supported until after the fact. The paranoid patient treated with supportive advice who feels manipulated or attacked or the obsessive-compulsive patient treated with supportive advice who feels controlled have been supported in theory but not in fact.

Some specific supportive techniques are the following:

1. Forming a substitute relationship. This is useful during periods of acute loss such as the loss of a person or of part of one's body (postsurgical). When the loss is of another person, a substitute relationship may tide the patient over loneliness. When it is of a body part, the therapist can be there to decrease grief and/or help correct false ideas about the loss. For example, a patient who lost both breasts in a mastectomy developed homosexual anxiety when she fantasized that she "now had the small breasts of a boy."

2. Teaching and giving advice. Here you tell a patient who is floundering what to do. One patient described it thusly: "I was like a turtle on its back, and you turned me over." Try to give advice in such a way that the patient believes he or she thought of it first. Lead the patient on to his or her own counsel. Advice is especially effective in the beginning of therapy, when the patient is floundering, and at the end of therapy, when the patient has much of the insight he or she needs and now is prepared for a little fatherly, motherly, or expert

advice. To deliberately misquote Adolf Meyer and Otto Kernberg, the patient is ready for common sense when therapy leaves off.

3. Discipline. Nonproductive or self-destructive behavior is discouraged or forbidden. The patient might say, "I'm sick so I can't help myself," to which you might reply, "I don't know if you can't or you won't, but you have to."

4. Structure. Just the presence of regularly occurring sessions can organize the patient's life. Many patients have been helped simply by being put on a schedule (be it weight-loss meetings, gym, or psychotherapy).

5. Enhancing self-esteem. A therapist enhances self-esteem by accepting the patient, telling the patient he or she is worthwhile, and feeling positive about the patient when others are criticizing and condemning him or her. Even the masochist who thrives on criticism may respond positively (a response kept secret so that he or she may still maintain the fantasy that the mistreatment or suffering continues).

Example. A therapist treating a patient with a paranoid personality disorder in supportive, covering therapy did discuss the mechanism of projection, pointed out the realistic distortions that projection produced, showed the patient his need to maintain isolation to minimize interpersonal hostility, advised him to identify any paranoid ideas he needed to maintain so that at least he might keep them to himself, and advised him to avoid situations that provoked intolerable anxiety. But the therapist avoided a discussion of the patient's forbidden, unacceptable, and intolerable homosexual wishes—wishes the therapist believed best kept hidden from the patient. He did not tell his in fact celibate patient, "You are a homosexual without knowing it." Instead, whenever the topic came up, the therapist said, "You are less of a homosexual than you believe yourself to be." This reassured the patient, avoided touching sore points, allowed healing repression, and increased self-esteem because the patient had always equated "being homosexual" with "being defective."

The patient's wife was encouraged to participate in the supportive approach. She was told, "Don't make mysterious moves for which your husband is unprepared. Always explain what you have in mind. This way you will stop disruptive fantasy before it gets out of control. Also reassure him that he is loved, accepted, and that you are not his enemy. For example, tell him, over and over that you are 'not your adversary.' "

Advantages

Immediate improvement can occur, with a feeling of well-being resulting from reduction of anxiety, loneliness, sense of despair, and feelings of isolation.

Disadvantages

Supportive therapy, generally believed benign, may produce more unanticipated complications than other forms of treatment. (Indeed, it is supportive techniques that, being more direct and overt, tend more often to misfire than such supposedly nonsupportive techniques as interpretation.)

1. Support, when it falsely presumes inability to change, is a belittling technique because it overlooks potential capacity. For this reason, supplement support

wherever possible with uncovering. You will be surprised how many patients with an emotional problem are capable of at least some degree of insightful change.

2. Supportive techniques can become counterproductive when therapy replaces living.

3. Support when withdrawn (as it sooner or later has to be) leads to a recurrence of problems—sometimes worse problems than before.

4. Support is sometimes less welcomed than feared. Unlike the thankful "turtle" mentioned above, some patients resent and fear direct assistance because it means being infantilized or controlled or because the "approach" is misinterpreted as a sexual one. The patient, even when his or her life is saved, may later resent and condemn the psychiatrist for the psychiatrist's intrusive ways.

Here are diagnosis-dependent ways in which support can misfire:

a. The schizoid patient may feel overwhelmed by the closeness.

b. The schizotypal patient, discovering the beliefs of the therapist who opens up (e.g., to share experiences), may use what he or she learns to satirize and otherwise villify the therapist. This may happen when the patient perceives the therapist as "coming from" either one of two extremes: excessively conservative/ square/ordinary or excessively odd/eccentric/peculiar.

c. The paranoid patient may both accuse the supportive therapist of being insincere and see the approach as an attack or seduction.

d. The borderline patient may merge with the supporter as if the supporter were a mother then, fearing being overwhelmed or losing identity, emerge explosively, devaluing the therapist, and suddenly and unexpectedly quitting treatment.

e. The depressed patient may believe the support given to be insufficient because it is too little too late.

f. The passive dependent patient may use support as an end in and of itself and fail to do further therapeutic work, for example, interpretive work.

g. The obsessive-compulsive patient may be uncertain whether he or she needs or wants the support. The patient may resent the control or may counterreact out of stubbornness.

h. The hysterical patient may see support as a seduction.

Shock Therapy

Advantages

Generally thought to be unsafe and cruel, shock is safe, kind, and effective when done correctly for a properly selected patient. Some clinicians believe ECT, or shock therapy, to be especially useful for the depressed patient who does not respond to drugs and psychotherapy.

Disadvantages

The considerable potential for abuse is beyond the scope of this text.

Environmental Manipulation

Because environmental manipulation should be part of an evaluation and treatment plan, it is better called environmental therapy.

Advantages

1. Changing the patient's environment not only can produce improvement as dramatic as a more direct treatment approach but can be easier to do, because the others are often healthier than the patient.

2. Developmental and behavioral information obtained from others assists with diagnosis and treatment.

3. You can help the patient deal directly with the cause of his or her reactive disorder. Too often the therapist fails to use common sense and act to fix what is obviously wrong. The example of the analyst who misunderstood her patient's reactions to the pounding overhead (described in chapter 10) serves here to illustrate how the appropriate intervention was not insight followed by more insight, but rather, encouraging the patient to call the police and file a lawsuit. There would have been plenty of time to resolve continuing problems with the patient's father.

Rule: When getting a patient out of trouble, distinguish between two kinds of patient: a patient in treatment who gets into trouble and a patient in trouble who gets into treatment.

Disadvantages

1. The patient can question our loyalty should he or she perceive we are taking sides.

2. Family members when seen without the patient present invariably misquote the therapist to the patient. Then it is difficult to convince the suspicious, hypersensitive patient that nothing harmful has been said behind his or her back. While there are in rare instances (e.g., the dangerous patient or the altruistic therapist who wishes to delay bad news) reasons to form pacts of secrecy with relatives, and to apologize to the patient later, as often as possible follow this rule: The therapist who sees a relative, especially one who calls unexpectedly or appears in the office unannounced, informs the relative before the conversation begins that he or she will repeat information to the patient even though the relative has asked the therapist not to.

3. Dependent patients who ask that we do things for them when they should be doing things for themselves can be infantilized. Psychopathic-antisocial patients often aspire to greater trouble once they know that their therapist will be available to bail them out.

Consultation with Another Professional

Advantages

Consultation is useful when
1. the patient asks for it, sometimes even when acting out is the reason for

the request—often the case for consultations requested by suspicious paranoids and splitting borderlines.

2. the therapist is having insurmountable countertransference difficulties with the patient.

3. the therapist needs more information on how to treat.

4. the therapy is stagnant or the patient is getting worse.

The therapist should experience no shame in asking for the consultation. The patient may be told that the field is too complex to be mastered by any one individual. And that two heads seem to be better than one.

The job of the consultant is of course to assist, not defeat, the therapist. For this reason a good consultant will, when possible, recommend that the patient return to treatment to resolve problems, which are often misunderstandings between patient and therapist. Only rarely will it be necessary to recommend another treatment or another therapist.

Disadvantages

None, unless the consultants are inspired not to consult but to do battle.

Chapter 7

Becoming Technically Proficient

Poor technique is a worthy companion to lack of psychological knowledge, self-serving behavior, and covert sadism. The best therapists follow, not idiosyncratic, but established procedure. They develop effective technical skills and use them humanely. They avoid the extremes of a psychotherapy that is correct, formal, stilted, and uncaring, on the one hand, and warm, inspired, but wrong, on the other.

In this chapter we describe some of the established techniques of psychotherapy. (It supplements the last chapter, which describes some of the different modes of psychotherapy.)

INTRODUCTORY REMARKS

The beginning therapist is advised to develop technical skills by selecting a few sessions every week and to reflect back on them with the following in mind:

1. Giving a technical name to each and every maneuver made during that session: asking yourself, Was that Advice? Manipulation? Clarification? Confrontation?

2. Asking, And what did I intend to accomplish by my remark, formulation, or manipulation? Was it Supportive? Educational? For the purpose of imparting insight?

3. Asking, And what did I actually accomplish? Did the patient respond positively, negatively, or was there no response? (Especially to be avoided is the assumption that a negative response is invariably a resistance that perversely proves the therapist's point.)

TECHNIQUES OF PSYCHOTHERAPY

Dealing with Problems of Motivation

You can deal with inadequate motivation and conflicts about being motivated but you cannot create motivation where motivation is absent. The therapist who tries to talk, cajole, beg, or order the nonmotivated patient to change—for the greater good, for his or her future well-being, or for the benefit of others—is often wasting time.

Dealing with inadequate motivation

Inadequate motivation can appear as not wanting to change, at least enough to expend the time, effort, and money that change requires.

Inadequate motivation can be *intrapsychic,* the result of too little anxiety. Increase anxiety and you increase motivation. You might increase anxiety by increasing guilt ("That's cruel!") or by arousing previously somnolent forbidden instincts by way of interpretation ("This latent homosexuality of yours seems always to be getting in your way"). Conversely, remove guilt, anxiety, and self-disgust too quickly and you decrease motivation for change.

Inadequate motivation can be *extrapsychic,* for example, the outcome of inappropriate, excessive support from relatives or society. Decrease this support and you increase motivation. If you can, deal with the wife who makes excuses for her alcoholic husband or, if you are a social psychiatrist, psychologist, social worker, or nurse, with the society that is excessively permissive about psychopathic behavior.

Dealing with conflicts about being motivated

You can resolve such motivational conflicts as guilt about change. Here apparent lack of motivation is really due to a fear of being motivated, for example because of fear of success or a masochistic need to continue to suffer.

Education

Teaching the patient how to be a patient—the therapeutic contract

1. Cause and cure. After a minimum of one to two, and a maximum of six, evaluative sessions, the therapist should tell the patient what he or she believes is wrong and how to go about fixing it. The therapist should not permit the

patient to make assumptions about what is wrong, keeping the patient in the dark. Instead, the therapist should clearly inform the patient (when true) that he or she has emotional problems and tell the patient what treatment is the approach of choice for handling these emotional problems. Give a name to the method to be used.

2. The basic rule. Teach the patient how to be in treatment. Do not assume the patient knows what to do and is uncooperative when he or she does not do what is expected. If the talking cure is indicated, the patient is told to say whatever comes to mind (not to free-associate, however, unless in analysis). Nothing should be left out. What comes to mind must be said no matter how embarrassing or seemingly trivial. Often two or more thoughts come to mind at the same time; a selection has to be made, but avoid always selecting central over peripheral, present over past, and clean over obscene.

3. The therapeutic alliance. Make it clear this is a joint effort. Discourage patient overpassivity and therapist overactivity. Strike a balance between an authoritarian relationship, such as that between teacher and student, and a colleague relationship. This way you retain both the strength of authority and the capacity to influence as a peer and associate.

Describing the process/course of therapy

1. Explaining the therapist's initial silence. Tell the patient you will be listening, sometimes silently, for long periods. This is not because of perversity, or ill will, but because at first you have little to say and will have little to say until you learn more.

During this time of initial "silence of wonderment" and throughout most of therapy, the therapist will comment only when he or she has something useful to say. There will not be a word-by-word, sentence-by-sentence antiphonal response. If the silence is broken at all, it might be to ask the patient to add comments on what the patient has heard himself or herself say.

2. Anticipating resistances. Advise the patient of problems expected to interfere with psychotherapy. These include resistances such as suppression due to guilt and shame, and the ability the patient has to defeat therapy if he or she is masochistically inclined.

3. Anticipating acting out. The therapist should explain acting out, warn the patient that acting out is counterproductive, and explain why.

4. Anticipating transference and "transference illness." An explanation is given so that the patient is not taken aback to discover that he or she is distorting the real therapist into what the patient wishes or fears the therapist to be.

5. Anticipating expected complications. Tell the patient that therapy might temporarily or even permanently make him or her worse.

One patient who learned how to relate got worse because he lost his protective isolation. The isolation protected him from the anxiety of relating; from depression, with attendant feelings of rejection and loss; and from paranoia, the result of projection (of forbidden instincts aroused by closeness).

6. Anticipating results. Tell the patient that therapy even if done properly with a motivated individual may yield few, if any, positive results. The patient should be forewarned that the usual favorable outcome is not "cure" but "more gain than loss." Therapy invariably involves a trade-off, so that the patient who gets better in some ways will get worse in other ways. For example, he or she might become less neurotic but also less spontaneous, and more superficial because of being less intense and missing the depth of character lent by conflict. Tell the patient whether you expect a little, some, or a great deal of improvement and not to be disappointed by anything short of a miracle. Tell the patient what form the improvement will take—such as diminished anxiety or obsessionalism.

7. Anticipating premature termination. The patient should be told that therapy is voluntary. Tell the patient that he or she is free to leave at any time, after giving appropriate notice and talking about the reasons for terminating.

8. Outlining the therapist's policies.

a. On fees and payment. The patient should be told the therapist's fee, his or her policy about insurance coverage (e.g., assignment), told when he or she is expected to pay, and in selected cases forewarned that delayed payment will provoke a discussion of delayed payment—a discussion that necessarily detracts from a discussion of the patient's problems.

b. On missed sessions, cancellations, and vacations. Discuss the therapist's policy about these in advance. All therapists should charge for missed sessions. Some therapists charge for canceled sessions even though adequate notice is given. Others do not if the reasons for the cancellation are believed sound, because it was unavoidable. It is often wise to request that the patient take vacations at the same time as the therapist if it is possible for the patient to do so. Otherwise the patient can schedule vacations not for rest and relaxation but as a resistance to treatment.

Giving advice

This includes the mundane—such as advice about health, nutrition, bad companions—as well as the transcendental—advice about spiritual matters, ideals, and so on. Attention to timing, focus, and critical implications are as important with giving advice as with clarification and interpretation. For example, many patients require some psychotherapy before they are able to accept advice otherwise perceived as competitive, controlling, or infantilizing.

Bad advice can result from lack of knowledge of the patient's dynamics. For example, a therapist who told his depressed patient that to feel better he needed to improve his external circumstances by making more money gave the wrong advice, and was perceived correctly as insensitive and ill-taken because this patient's depression rested more on spiritual than on mundane factors.

It is sometimes best to avoid giving direct advice. It is sometimes a bit reckless to put oneself in the position of being responsible for another's life. Since everyone is different, can even the experienced, learned therapist have all the necessary information to make decisions for another? The therapist who makes decisions for a patient or tells the patient what to do should ask him- or herself who is to be responsible if the advice sours. And many patients, when feeling negative toward us (as all must sooner or later feel), will create a disaster for themselves simply to punish the therapist. Thus one patient allowed himself to be guided into one medical field rather than another; the thinking was rational and the conclusion sensible based on the patient's presentation. But the patient withheld information so that he could be angry for having been pushed around, then punished his perceived controller by defeating himself in the chosen field.

Keeping in mind that there are exceptions (discussed below and elsewhere), try to lead the patient to his or her own conclusions. Discuss alternatives and point out advantages and disadvantages. Then tell the patient, "The decision is yours; you make it, and I will help you with it once you have made it." Thus one patient, ambivalent about marrying a man who loved her but whom she believed to be too old to appeal to her sexually, repeatedly asked the therapist, "What shall I do?" and was repeatedly told, "The decision is yours to make; it has to be, for no one can make it for you. But *after* you make it, *then* I will help you implement it, live with it, or change it if it doesn't seem to be working out."

Part of treatment is trying out the alternatives. See which are more appealing, practical, and rewarding. Any anxiety aroused can be handled by reassurance or interpretation. For example, one patient, a masochist, was told to try "feeding himself a little pleasure." The therapist suggested, "Start simply with such activities as pleasure walks and shopping." When anxiety appeared, it was interpreted as the result of fear of success, in turn the result of fear of hurting the father.

We might make exceptions to the rule in the following situations (but even these patients retain some underlying resentment of being told what to do, know how another person cannot make decisions for them, and prefer to make their own decisions when possible): (a) the regressed schizophrenic, helpless without leadership; (b) the anxiously ambivalent, paralyzed obsessional; (c) the passive, dependent patient, not effectively motivated on his or her own; (d) the mildly to severely confused patient; (e) the unknowledgeable patient, for example, the patient protected for all his or her life, or new to the culture.

Below is an example of good advice and an example of bad.

Good advice. A blind patient developed an identity as a blind athlete. He became a gym instructor, who, unable to instruct, entertained the clients by telling them jokes. He also ran marathons for charity without attracting much attention or money. This compensatory behavior, while it enabled him to feel more whole, in fact produced little income and led nowhere. His therapist convinced him to accept his limitations and attend school for the blind, receiving training in an appropriate field. Eventually he became a successful businessman.

Bad advice. A depressed, masochistic dental student wanted to be a saxophone player but was convinced by his parents to go to dental school because "there you can always make a living." In the beginning he hated dental school but adapted and came to love dental research. His parents forced him to see a therapist believing he was about to ruin himself financially unless he entered private practice. To retaliate and render the treatment ineffective, he deliberately selected a therapist perceived to be incompetent. But he did not count on the power of the transference. Under its spell he believed the therapist knew what was best. Alas, the therapist, without taking a family history, repeated the parental admonition to "go into private practice because that's where all the money is." The dentist became a technically effective practitioner but unhappy and overcontrolling with his own patients.

Sharing Experiences

The therapist tells the patient how he or she might react, behave, and/or resolve problems under similar circumstances. Sharing experiences is not only educative but helps the patient who resists because he or she thinks of the therapist as one who is not sick, "so how can he (or she) understand me?"

Heed the following warnings about this appealing therapeutic technique: (a) Only talk about yourself when relevant, not when a product of self-interest and narcissism; (b) don't be presumptuous. Not all of your solutions are suitable for your patients. There are other approaches besides yours; (c) do not overdo sharing experiences when the patient fears getting too close because of paranoia (so suspicious of hostile or sexual motives) and when the patient fears getting too close because of being borderline (so afraid of loss of identity).

Unlearning Learned Guilt

Guilt that is learned can be unlearned, by exhortation, example, and identification with the therapist. But decreasing guilt can be ill-considered for narcissistic or psychopathic patients who allow themselves to get things they do not deserve, either because they have not worked for them or because they belong to someone else.

Philosophical Teaching

Example: A patient believed that it is wiser to keep your mouth shut and let people think you were a fool than to open it up and make them certain that you were a fool. He was told that the formulation, though appealing, was not only sophistic but that the idea people would think him a fool was an incorrect primary postulate (from low self-esteem) upon which his version of the clever maxim was too facilely constructed.

Support

What different therapists mean by the term was discussed in chapter 6. Often the term is used to denote a technique opposite on the continuum from expressive-insight techniques. But almost any technique can be supportive, even expressive insight. It depends on therapist intent and patient response as much as any inherent quality of the technique. Thus interpretation can be supportive when the therapist intends to show the patient something flattering about him- or herself. Or the depressed patient may even feel supported by criticism if he or she believes suffering is cleansing.

The tolerance, interest, and concern of any good psychotherapist is supportive because it improves the patient's self-esteem. For example, the patient might think, If the therapist is interested, then I must be interesting. Or the patient might think, If you are worried about me professionally, then I must be important enough to worry about.

Short-term support, a form of crisis intervention, is useful for the reactive disorders such as pathological grief, reactive depression, and schizophreniform disorder.

Abreaction

Encourage the patient to talk, and be willing to listen. Tell the patient, "Don't be ashamed. I've heard everything before." Tell the patient of your tolerance, that you will find him or her acceptable even with his or her problems. Because many patients omit material they think not interesting enough to mention, tell the patient that you find even the most routine data important and (one hopes) interesting. Because interjections, comments, and interpretations can interfere, try not to interrupt unless you have specific questions about what the patient has said.

Clarification

Clarification simply means "making clear." Here are some examples of clarification: (a) The therapist edits the patient's productions so that they are comprehensible to both the therapist and the patient; (b) the therapist removes such impurities as digressions from the patient's productions; (c) the therapist grasps a peripheral matter and thrusts it to center stage; (d) the therapist confirms a suspicion.

There are several considerations in giving clarifications: (a) timing—premature clarifications may be neither heard nor understood; (b) selection of focus—the therapist faced with a number of possibilities will select the one best suited to accomplish his or her therapeutic goal; (c) critical aspects—the therapist may have to edit the clarification to soften its critical impact. The patient's own ideas, even the patient's own words, take on a brutal, stark, punitive quality when heard coming from the mouth of the therapist. Often the critical implication of a clarification can be softened by approaching the matter from the side of a fear rather than of a wish. For example, the therapist might say, "It appears to me from what you say that you are troubled by your anger," rather than "You seem angry?"

Some approaches though "clarificatory" are conventionally called by another name. As an example, we identify the patient's problems by giving them a name, an organizing handle. This "clarification" we call diagnosis. Another example is clarification by taking a history, as follows:

Clarification by taking a history

A good history underlines the important events in the patient's life. Connections appear between events until now believed unrelated. Insight often follows. (We also interpret by creating new connections.)

Organization of the history. A history should be organized according to identifying data, chief complaint, present illness (or, for the nonmedically oriented, chief problem and present disorder), past history, family history, and social history.

1. Identifying data. This should include age, sex, and marital status, and when appropriate other data, such as number of children and job status. Example: a 37-year-old white married mother of four.

2. Chief complaint or chief problem. This is a statement of the problem *in the patient's own words* and from his or her point of view. An example of a chief complaint is, "I'm depressed because my husband is leaving me," not, "Reactive depression." Another example (given by a schizophrenic patient merely repeating what his therapist told him) is, "I need treatment to avoid being in a back ward someday." A third, also given by a schizophrenic patient, is, "I don't want to be backwards." Include, where appropriate, the *duration* of the chief complaint. For example, "My husband asked for a divorce about a year and a half ago, and I've been depressed since then."

3. Present illness. This elaborates the chief complaint descriptively, developmentally, and dynamically. It incorporates relevant facts from the past (psychological/medical) history, social history, and family history. In the above case of the patient whose husband was leaving her, the therapist decided to include the divorce of the patient's parents in the present illness when he learned that the patient's mother at the time of her own divorce, was the same age as the patient's present age.

Here is a more extensive example of how a patient's *past (medical) history* and *family history* can properly belong in the present illness (disorder):

A patient developed a post-traumatic stress disorder (the "chief complaint") after the following incident. She was shopping in an appliance store when a former employee entered, brandishing a gun, took hostages, then began shooting, killing two hostages and wounding several more. The patient saw the dead bodies on the floor, bleeding. She tried to escape from the back of the store but was trapped because the door was bolted shut.

Her present trauma revived two earlier traumata: a traumatic tonsillectomy at age 2 and a traumatic spontaneous abortion several years ago when she lost the son she always wanted to have. The latter loss contributed a distinct depressive strain to the present illness.

When the patient was 6 years old, her father's brother shot and killed himself in the patient's presence.

Here is an example of how *dynamic evaluation* of the chief complaint properly belongs in the patient's present illness.

The schizophrenic patient who said, "I don't want to be backward," condensed into his plaint three significant wishes/fears: (1) the wish not to be schizophrenic, (2) the wish not to be of low intelligence, (3) the wish not to be homosexual (there was a special meaning for him of *back* in *backward*).

4. Past history. Include here emotional problems whose relevance to the present illness may not be immediately apparent and/or may be of uncertain relationship to the present illness.

5. Family history. Look for evidence of hereditary cause. Look for evidence of provocation: ask if the patient gets worse when provoked by family members. (Do not forget to ask the patient if he or she gets better when supported by or ignored by them.) Search for losses: help the patient to remember often forgotten losses of important relationships and often forgotten losses of siblings who died at birth.

6. Social history. How does the patient function at work, in nonfamily interactions, and in love?

Interpretation

Clarification versus interpretation

Though they overlap, a clarification may be said to enlighten by reorganizing/reemphasizing the already known, while in contrast an interpretation introduces the patient to the previously unknown, for example, by making new connections, or by making the unconscious conscious. A simple example (from literature): The emperor has no clothes. Everyone knew (preconsciously), but no one recognized (consciously), that the emperor was naked.

Danger

Because most preconscious/unconscious material is such because it is unpalatable (e.g., anxiety-provoking), timing, focus, and softening of brutality can be even more important for interpretations than for clarifications. Accurate (and some inaccurate) interpretation when premature, if not rejected, may also provoke acting out (in an attempt to avoid frightening material or to punish the therapist) or may cause regression, even a psychotic break.

Example. A woman who believed her male companion mistreated her in fact provoked him. She complained excessively about his clothing and weight, criticized his family, and mercilessly put him down for telling off-color jokes. She thought, not, I am being impossible, but rather, If he loved me, he would change his clothes, drop his family, and stop telling dirty jokes. The therapist suggested her neurosis led her to mistreat him the same way her mother mistreated her father. Her response was not, "Eureka, thank you," but, "Even you, my own therapist, don't take my side," and, "If I'm like my mother this way, how else am I like her (Oedipal anxiety)?" Naturally she interrupted therapy. She then found a therapist who avoided taking sides and comparing her to her mother by this simple technique: he sympathized with her difficulties. He said only, "It must be hard for you in this difficult relationship." This calmed the patient. And as soon as she no longer felt attacked and criticized, she herself volunteered how she was provocative.

Wild analysis

A mixture of accurate and inaccurate interpretations given in a random, shotgun fashion is called wild analysis. In addition to anxiety, such therapy often provokes disorganization and massive regression.

Special problems

a. Overinterpretation in the schizophrenic. The schizophrenic patient is often made worse by uncovering techniques. For example, it is better to tell some schizophrenics, "You are not as angry as you think," instead of, "You will not be surprised to learn how you are flooded with anger."

b. Problems with interpretation in the obsessive-compulsive patient. Interpretations are superfluous because without affect there is no effect. The patient knows his or her unconscious only too well as it is revealed in preoccupations that torture the patient but have no emotional impact so do not hit home. For example, a patient was tortured by homosexual thoughts about his doctor. Yet he averred, "I'm not a homosexual—I have no homosexual desires." The therapist showed the obsessive-compulsive patient who feared leaving a dirty cup behind (see below) that his forbidden hostile and sexual impulses were at the root of his concern. The *fear* of contamination was interpreted as a *wish* to have sexual contact and a wish to contaminate and kill others. The patient seemed delighted with the insight, and "analyzed all my rituals according to what you just told me, Doc." But there was no real feeling, and the patient remained intellectually detached. The rituals continued, and after two days the interest in the self-analysis waned. (Treatment of the obsessive-compulsive patient consists less of undoing repression than of diminishing guilt, in this way restoring isolated feeling, needed for true understanding.) ·

Interpretation of the transference

The therapist focuses on the patient's disorder as it is repeated in the therapeutic relationship. To paraphrase Freud's statement made in the context of understanding dreams, this is a royal road to the unconscious. But informational advantages are counterbalanced by the following disadvantages:

a. Excessive preoccupation with transference may lead to failure to deal with matters in the here and now. The patient may lose touch with daily reality—especially disruptive for some tenuously related borderline patients.

b. Fostering therapy as a way of life, as in the following case:

A therapist suggested to a couple in difficulty that they come to her five times a week. Outside of sessions they could continue to live together but were forbidden to talk to one another. In sessions they were to discuss "your fantasies about me." Analysis of the fantasies was to dispel neurosis and create marital harmony. Instead the patients became a casualty of treatment, excessively preoccupied with abnormal psychology, problem solving, and their thoughts, not about each other, but about the therapist.

Short-term analysis

This is especially useful for maturational crises unresolvable because of Oedipal fixation. An advantage of short-term uncovering (interpretive) techniques is that with proper selection of patients, the therapist can avoid complications such as dependent and sadomasochistic transference and prolonged artificial living. Two disadvantages are that work is necessarily incomplete and the patient, given a termination date, may anticipate abandonment actively so that he or she does not experience it passively. This is one reason for a flight into health.

Working Through

Fallacy: There is a special time for working through.

Fact: This should be an ongoing activity.

Fallacy: We work through only new-found *insight*.

Fact: We have to work through any new piece of information—exhortation and advice as well as insight. Only by applying and reapplying something do we finally make it part of our automatic behavior.

Cognitive Techniques

In chapter 6 it was discussed how cognitive therapy primarily recognizes and treats thought process and thought content disorder. We contrast an analytic, pharmacotherapeutic, and cognitive approach: An *analyst* might treat paranoid personality disorder by identification of the anxiety that promotes projection, for example, fear of one's forbidden hostile instincts or forbidden sexual instincts. A *pharmacotherapist* might give antipsychotic agents to influence projective thinking by decreasing this anxiety. A *cognitive* therapist might identify, discuss, and discourage the projective thinking itself.

Examples of disordered thought content and process in the different diagnostic categories are the following:

Schizophrenia. Dreamlike (primary process), with disregard for logic and such reality as the reality of time relationships.

Paranoia. Projective thinking, the tendency to disavow "me" and reattribute it to "you."

Borderline. Devaluing-overvaluing thinking, the tendency to love or hate, with nothing in between.

Depressive. All-is-lost thinking, the tendency to make mountains out of molehills.

Anxiety. Fear thinking, or the tendency to react with alarm to one's own instincts when they are believed correctly or incorrectly to be forbidden.

Phobic. Trivial prompt thinking, or the tendency to displace internal anxiety onto an external object, such as a dog or bridge. The external object, inherently unimportant, becomes a symbol that activates anxiety or panic.

Obsessive-compulsive. Doing and undoing thinking, or salving one's conscious by taking back what you just thought, said, or did.

Psychopathic. Sly thinking, or the tendency to justify one's preconceived conclusions by false logic, especially when for immediate personal gain. In a thought process/content disorder that is the opposite of overinclusiveness, the psychopath omits ideas that run contrary to the self-serving point he or she wishes to make.

Narcissistic. Self-centered thinking, or emphasizing everything from the "me" angle.

Masochistic. Self-punitive thinking, for example, the tendency to believe that if it is bad for me, then it is good for me.

Sadistic. Other-punitive thinking, for example, the tendency to believe that if it is bad for you, it is good for you.

Behavioral Techniques

Manipulation

Here the therapist plans a special effect, often perverse. An example is reverse psychology, whereby the therapist gets a stubborn patient to do the therapist's bidding by ordering the patient to do the opposite of what is intended. Another example is manipulation through flattery.

An advantage is the potential for direct, rapid influence on manifest behavior. Three disadvantages are that it (1) bypasses formative dynamics, so the problem may recur; (2) is an inexact science so can misfire and have the reverse effect of what the therapist intends as in the following example:

One patient, unable to get to class on time because he slept through the alarm, was told, "don't set the alarm, sleep late" (reverse psychology). As anticipated, he arose on time "waiting for the clock to go off," then, having nothing to do, went to class, arriving promptly. But then, feeling manipulated, and to spite the therapist, he either fell asleep in class or, after paying close attention, both forgot what he heard and lost his lecture notes.

And (3) premature removal of a needed symptom can create intolerable anxiety. Symptom return or replacement, perhaps worse than before, may result.

Setting limits

Limits may be set to control or stop the patient's unpleasant, self-defeating, or dangerous nontransferential and transferential behavior, the latter sometimes for the good of the therapist (all therapists have limits to their patience and tolerance).

The following is an example of nontransferential behavior that had to be stopped:

A patient lived in an apartment the windows of which were being fixed. The patient did not want the workmen to see into his apartment. Having only transparent shades, he blocked the view by stringing sheets of paper towel on the windows.

The following is an example of transferential behavior (controlling intolerable transference overinvolvement) that had to be stopped:

The above-mentioned obsessive-compulsive patient began to involve the therapist in his pre- and post-therapy bathroom rituals. For example, he might knock on the therapist's door before a session to tell the therapist that the clean cups were about to run out. Or he might have to be buzzed in again after a session when he returned to the office to check to see if the toilet had stopped running. The therapist responded directly by saying, "You may continue to torture yourself if you like, but I won't permit your interrupting my concentration, my work, even torturing me."

Both positive and negative behaviors might require limit-setting (whether or not they are a product of emotional disorder, i.e., unplanned, unwanted, and unrecognized).

Examples of the positive include erotomanic and dependent behaviors. Example of the negative include homicidal, masochistic (especially when harm to self is more real than symbolic), suicidal, bizarre, acting out/impulsive, antisocial (by *antisocial* is meant immoral and/or of questionable legality), illegal, asocial (withdrawn) and anhedonic behaviors.

When you tell the patient to stop, do so kindly, and add self-esteem enhancement to undo implied criticism. Thus one self-destructive, homosexual patient, told, "I forbid you to pick up one more person from the street," was also told, "Because often these people aren't good enough for you, and you deserve to meet nice people in nice places."

There are at least three ways to set limits:

(1) Directly—by direct interdiction. The therapist asks the patient to stop. On

the negative side, this is more easily said than done when it amounts to asking the patient to abandon the very problem that requires treatment so that the patient may get the treatment he or she needs. Yet the therapist must avoid being overly subtle or coy, in this way unconsciously aligning him- or herself with the patient's tendency toward self-destruction. On the positive side, you will not be telling the patient to do something he or she does not already know must be done. And even if the patient only thinks twice about his or her behavior, or stops a little instead of a lot, matters are often improved enough both to permit life to be more satisfying and creative and to permit further therapeutic work to proceed unhampered.

Some patients need to be told to discuss each and every activity with the therapist before they take any action at all. The therapist who tells the patient to discuss everything first is of course not bound to respond to each discussion with advice and suggestions. The therapist may simply monitor behavior to intervene selectively. In contrast, some patients are advised to discuss selected areas only, for example, the spending of money. Selectivity is of special importance in those patients who are both impulsive and paralyzed. One obsessive-compulsive patient agonized literally for days about the cheapest way to send a package, then in one day invested hundreds of thousands of dollars in a stock market mutual fund, merely on the strength of the reputation of the manager.

It is always unwise for the patient to inform the world (as some patients do) that action is postponed until the patient can speak with his or her therapist. Such a matter is between the therapist and the patient. Another reason for delay can be given friends and family, lest the patient seem overly dependent, overly infantile, or bizarre.

(2) Indirectly—by treating the underlying problem, for example, by relieving the anxiety, guilt, or affective disorder at the root of the impulsivity. Thus the patient who tries one sexual partner after another may do so impulsively for a reason: because he or she feels basically unloved, empty, and depressed.

(3) By time delay. The therapist asks the patient to maintain the status quo that exists at the moment (unless intolerable). The therapist says, "Don't do anything for a certain period of time. Let's talk for six months or so, then you can make decisions." This is a compromise approach, one that tells the patient what to do ("do nothing for now" is, after all, a kind of suggestion), while at the same time not telling him or her what to do.

Example. A borderline patient who could not wait to devalue her mate was told, "It will wait. You can tell him him off next week. What's the rush? For now, don't say a thing. Let's explore your feelings."

Example. A newspaper reporter, unable to decide whether to keep his full-time job or go freelance, alternated between quitting and staying on his job until he drove his boss and his wife to distraction. Finally, he quit his job. But then he tried to get it back again. He went part-time as a compromise, then quit his part-time position. This patient should have been told in the beginning, not, "The decision is yours," not, "Quit," not "Don't quit," but, "Don't quit your job for a year." The reason for this advice should have been given as, ''This gives us time to study the problem.'' The patient might have thus been spared his embarrassing, painful, humiliating behavior.

Secondary behavioral intervention

Even techniques such as clarification and interpretation owe a part of their effect to behavioral mechanisms. For example, the therapist can condition by way of selection or nonselection of topic.

Chapter 8

Long-Term Insight-Oriented Therapy

Speaking of analysis, Freud likened the process of treatment to a chess game and drew an analogy between teaching the beginner how to play chess and how to do therapy. He noted that in both cases the opening and closing moves are more easily described than the moves to be made in the middle "game," where art more often than not replaces science.

We will describe the three phases of long-term insight-oriented psychotherapy and some of the techniques used in each of these phases.

Therapists regardless of orientation can benefit somewhat from the material in this chapter, for each patient's therapy, no matter how brief and no matter what the mode, should be structured roughly according to the triphasic model presented here. Even pharmacotherapy has three phases: the first phase, in which the problem is outlined; the middle phase, in which data are gathered and integrated, and the final phase, a summing up, formulation, presentation of a treatment plan, and a working-through (e.g., adjustment of medication).

THE OPENING PHASE

Beginning

Waiting list and initial contact

Therapy can begin even before the first face-to-face contact. It can begin with the initial referral or when the patient has been officially put on the waiting list for treatment. Just knowing of the possibility of a future ongoing, possibly stable relationship provides promise of relief from loneliness and isolation, promise of an activity that might reduce boredom, the self-esteem-enhancing idea that another cares in a generally positive way, and the promise of improvement in the future.

Opening the first session

The first words: One therapist chose to open the first session with every patient by asking, "What would you like to have me do to help you?" The therapist who asks this inspired question poses a powerful contradiction to a typical distortion most patients have. They distort the real reason for coming. "I have problems you might solve" becomes, "I am forced to be here; you are forcing me to do something you want me to do; I am here not for my benefit but for your benefit, and for the benefit of my relatives and friends." Even the voluntary patient who comes in on his or her own or who is referred by request can think this way.

Getting to know one another

The therapist who reveals him- or herself, for example waxing ecstatic about not having personal problems ("Yes, I can relieve your fears by assuring you that I have a wife and kids") is just as inappropriate as the therapist with problems who chooses to unburden him- or herself about them to the patient. The prying patient should be reminded that (1) therapy is a technique that can be practiced equally well by different people with different life-styles and with different personal problems and (2) discussing the therapist's personal life is more often than not a way of avoiding the job at hand, which is discussing the patient's personal life.

How to instruct the patient to reveal him- or herself to the therapist (the basic rule, with modifications) was discussed in chapter 7.

Giving immediate assistance

Rule 1. Even if you are a hands-off analyst, offer to extend a helping hand to the patient who is extremely uncomfortable, or in trouble, especially when in danger. Offer when the patient has no one else (especially the case for isolated, schizoid patients), fails to realize the need for help (because of being uninsightful or masochistic), is unwilling or afraid to help him- or herself (because of being masochistic or phobic with a fear of success), or is too unknowledgeable to ask for and get the help needed.

Rule 2. Never refuse immediate help under the guise of refusing to contaminate the transference. (Many analysts and other therapists who officially say they refuse to contaminate the transference unofficially do otherwise—or else they would have no practice.)

How long should the therapist wait before making clarifications and interpretations?

There are two schools of thought:

1. In the beginning stages of treatment, some therapists exercise interpretative restraint. They tell the patient that they will at first listen silently, explain that it might be some time before they have anything useful to say, and ask the patient's indulgence, asking the patient to realize that it takes time to understand another person. The therapist requests patience so there is no pressure to say something that will later be found to be prematurely said, or erroneous.

2. Equally careful therapists use clarification and interpretation early in treatment. They believe that even though you have to learn a great deal about the patient before you can say or do much that is accurate/inclusive, the necessarily tentative, inexact, or even incorrect clarifications and interpretations given at this stage can be revised later on. Meanwhile they at least help isolate and focus the patient's problems for the therapist and the patient. And they believe partial understanding is better than no understanding at all.

The therapist should proceed with inexact formulations only after reassuring him- or herself that (1) the patient can appreciate how tentative the formulations are; (2) if productive of premature closure, the material can be rescued once again; (3) the inexactness after being corrected would not be used against the therapist in a negative way or against the patient, by the patient, in a self-defeating manner. As an example of a self-defeating, therapist-defeating response, one patient held the therapist to something he said early in therapy and refused to accept the revision in the service of having a "masochistic triumph."

Getting informed consent

This should be obtained (verbal or written) even though the patient is voluntary and does not seem suspicious, litigious, and so on. Possible failures, complications, and the like should be discussed. Although complications involving drugs are usually discussed, complications of psychotherapy are rarely given the same attention, possibly because of the incorrect belief that psychotherapy is not a powerful tool and so will have few meaningful complications.

The therapist may want to take notes on or record the proceedings.

Educating the patient on how to do therapy

Teaching the patient how to do therapy was discussed in chapter 7.

Injunctions

1. Reading. Some therapists discourage the patient from reading about his or her therapy believing that the patient will use the information in the service of resistance. Others encourage it, believing that the patient might learn something useful for his or her treatment.

2. Silence about treatment outside of treatment. Stricter therapists ask the

patient not to discuss treatment outside of treatment. Less strict therapists permit this as long as the discussion is brought back into the therapy, not lost. The patient may be told that to do otherwise is to water the therapeutic soup, creating more of it to go around, but a brew less pungent and effective.

3. Note taking (by the patient). Ask the patient not to write things down. Writing down dreams is fruitless (see below); writing down reactions to internal and external events, and/or planning the session ahead, is stultifying as well as fruitless. (One patient had the whole session planned, including the desired therapist response. He sketched in where the therapist might speak, and allowed what the therapist might say. The therapist was permitted little else other than to reassure the patient that he had not done something to "completely ruin his life.")

4. Delaying decision making. (See also the discussion of time delay, under the section "Setting limits" in chapter 7.) Some therapists ask their patients not to make decisions for a while, or until therapy is over. This seemingly innocuous injunction in fact can be powerful, perhaps dangerous, when used inappropriately. It can stall an already paralyzed obsessional, intensify loss of interest in an already anhedonic depressive, and so on.

5. Abstinence. A patient semihumorously described his feelings about treatment as "taking the vows of poverty [because of the fee], chastity [because of the role of sexual abstinence in his treatment], and obedience [because of the perceived control exercised by his therapist]." While some analyses—for example, of sexual symptoms such as ego-dystonic homosexuality—best occur with the patient abstinent, other forms of treatment require hands off, or the reverse—that is, increased sexual activity is recommended (e.g., sexual exploration, surrogates).

Forms of abstinence not primarily sexual may be complete avoidance of another—for example, a spouse—or limited avoidance of another—for example, a spouse except for business discussions and couple therapy in the therapist's office.

6. No acting out. Acting out relieves tension needed for fantasy buildup. Because fantasy is used for many forms of treatment (e.g., analytic, cognitive), acting out should be discouraged for itself because the patient can get into trouble and because it interferes with the therapeutic process. The therapist who is not using fantasy may be less chagrined by the patient's acting out, stopping it when it becomes dangerous more than when it represents a repetition that avoids an understanding of the problem for which the patient professes to seek treatment.

Listing the manifest problems

List the problems your patient has aloud. Does the patient have the following:

1. Symptoms—such as depression, physical problems caused by emotions, or physical problems appearing in the mental sphere such as an organic brain disorder?

2. Pathological affects such as pathological euphoria or depression?

3. Excessive anxiety—that warning signal of excessive guilt or potential flooding, with attendant decompensation?

4. Excessive defensiveness? Examples include excessive regression, denial, projection.

5. Interpersonal problems? Examples are schizoid removal, self-defeating (rather than self-fulfilling) behavior, and selfish (rather than altruistic) behavior.

6. Problems of daily living, such as problems at work?

THE MIDDLE PHASE

In-depth Evaluation of Structural/Dynamic Problems

When possible, a problem should be understood using genetic, organic, analytic (developmental/dynamic), behavioral, and cognitive models simultaneously. For example, one depression seemed all of these: genetic because it was inherited from the mother; organic because of hormones (worse premenstrually); developmental because it was the product of oral fixation; dynamic because it was the product of a defense (introjection of guilty anger); behavioral because it was a conditioned response, with depression rewarded by maternal concern; and cognitive because it was the product of alarmist thinking—that is, any intimation of mild interpersonal tension was invariably interpreted as total rejection.

Here are some of the problems to identify and evaluate:

1. Reactive problems—such as a depression resulting from a bad marriage and/or self-made—imagined and fantastic, such as one hysteric's frigidity, the result of the belief that every man she met was "just like my father."

2. Disparity between the ego and the ego ideal. Many problems are fundamentally problems of self-realization. Depression (as Bibring [1953] pointed out) can result in part because the patient cannot meet the standards he or she has set for him- or herself. Align self-expectation and accomplishment and this aspect of the problem disappears. One may either raise the level of accomplishment or, with caution, lower the standards. For example, a patient too dependent on success at work as measured by recognition from his boss learned to be satisfied with success at home, as measured by recognition from his family and friends. Another patient learned to be satisfied with self-satisfaction and self-congratulations, to not measure success by what others thought of him.

3. Ego weakness due to the impairment of one or more functions of the ego. Examples of ego dysfunction, consequences of dysfunction (implied or stated), and some treatment hints follow: a. Incapacity for insight. A well-functioning ego can "split itself in two" and observe itself (observant ego).

b. Inadequacy of defense. The defense mechanisms may be inadequate to the task of mastering anxiety. An example is what happens in some schizophrenia:

an inadequate capacity for repression allows threatening material to appear in the patient's consciousness, with the result that the patient is overwhelmed with anxiety.

c. Maladaptive defense. Defenses are maladaptive when they are too primitive (regression), used too excessively (persistent reaction formation), or are productive of reality-testing impairment (as below).

d. Impairment of reality testing. Misperception and misunderstanding of reality and failure to sort internal from external reality are aspects of the inability to reality test. Defensive maneuvers such as denial and projection are often psychotic because, though they reduce anxiety, they simultaneously distort reality.

Not all impairment of reality testing is psychotic, as in the following example:

This patient's obsessionalism in great part resulted from contamination of external by internal reality (fantasy.) He feared assertion because in fantasy it meant murder. One result was that whenever this patient wrote an assertive letter, for example, a letter of complaint, he saw his assertion as aggression, became guilty about his aggression, then expressed the guilt as a fear that he had written a death threat. Even an assertive compliment became an aggressive criticism (i.e., a death threat; after writing a letter to the president of the United States heartily complimenting him on a job well done, he worried about the possibility that he had threatened to kill the president and would be caught and punished. For days after sending the letter, the patient feared that the Feds would come to his door and take him away).

An important nondefensive instance of inability to reality test is the tendency to confuse a wish with a deed (a form of magical thinking). Obsessionals in particular believe that a thought is to be condemned as much as, and like, an action. Such patients need to be repeatedly reminded that thinking is not the same thing as doing.

While the therapist most often assists patients to perceive reality correctly, sometimes the therapist assists the patient to distort, not perceive, reality. When perception is too harsh and realistic without fantasy, the therapist may help the patient create fantasy. For example, depressed patients may be depressed because they have no fantasies left, are overly burdened by harsh reality, and, say, cannot fall asleep because they can not think the pleasant thoughts that most of us need to lull ourselves to sleep. Here the therapist creates, not reality from fantasy, but the other way around.

4. Management (sorting, organizing, blending). The ego as the manager of diverse, often antagonistic trends forges compromises, either symptomatic or creative. It is the therapist's job to undo some of the more pathological compromises and help the patient create better ones.

5. Future orientation. The ego has the ability to fix a point in the future and direct its efforts there. (Defensive functions are required to suppress awareness of a bleak future and/or awareness of the inevitability of death.)

Handling Resistances

The following are truisms about resistances:

1. All patients are resistant because all patients have an understandable reluctance to abandon primary and secondary gain. In other words, there is an inertialike tendency of neurotic or psychotic illness to maintain itself—for, after all, if the patient did not need and want the illness, if the illness did not serve a purpose, why develop it in the first place.

2. Resistances originate from negative and positive transference. The patient who does not like the therapist or who is so in love that therapy becomes a casualty of romance is said to be resistant. Handling specific negative and positive transference resistance is discussed in chapter 11.

3. Resistances are the manifestation of the operation of one or more defense mechanisms. The denying patient will deny problems, the repressing patient will forget problems, and the projecting patient will attribute problems to others. Handling defenses is discussed in chapter 9.

Resistances may be treated like all other material—cajoled away, charmed away, forbidden, analyzed, and so on. Rule: An important difference between resistances and all other material is that resistances often have to be treated first, otherwise there is no other material.

Imparting Knowledge (Insight)

Some general aspects of insight-oriented therapy were discussed in chapter 6, and some aspects of techniques for imparting insight were discussed in chapter 7. Here we ask and answer several questions about insight.

What is insight?

The macroscopic term *insight* covers the many microscopic processes required to identify the extent and scope of illness and to answer six questions about emotional illness: how, when, what, why, who, and where?

A patient with recurrent obscene obsessional thoughts and a door-checking compulsion that invariably made him late for work in the middle phase of treatment learned *how* his obsessions and compulsions were formed (e.g., they originated in identification with an obsessive-compulsive father and expressed submission to a seductive mother); *when* they began (he was able to identify an obsessive-compulsive tic—the need to touch each of his fingers in succession with his thumb, followed by the need to begin again—as early as the age of 2 years); *what* (which) of his present behaviors could be subsumed under the rubric of *obsessive* and *compulsive* (typically, he believed his obsessive concerns to be legitimate ego-syntonic worries and his compulsive, ritualistic behaviors sensible products of his free will); *why* early fears, forbidden wishes, and so on, contributed to his later symptomatic behaviors (his anxiety now was the same as his anxiety then, even though inappropriate now and even though now he was a big, strong adult, better able to cope than the small, weak child of then); *who* was involved in his illness (both the participants in his early disorder and the people in his present life who created, provoked, or aggravated his obsessionalism—including his parents even now, excessively controlling superiors at work, and a critical wife); and *where* his problems occurred (he learned how his obsessions and compulsions were provoked in one setting but not another; in his case he was free from obsessions at work because he hated his job but burdened with them at home because he loved his family).

Can you combine other techniques with insight-oriented techniques?

Do not think that an insight-oriented approach per se excludes cognitive, behavioral, or pharmacotherapeutic approaches. For example, for the depressed patient who thinks depressive thoughts and so creates a depressive affect, then finds that his or her depressive affect further encourages depressive thinking, a combination approach (cognitive, insight-oriented, pharmacotherapeutic) may be used. Indeed, all psychoanalyses employ cognitive approaches. Even the most analytically oriented therapist is likely to tell his or her patient, "You are making mountains out of molehills," or, "You see things in black and white but never in shades of gray."

How do you develop insight?

The process of insight therapy may be described simply as follows: get the patient talking and listen to what he or she says; tell him or her what you are learning, and learn together; then convert intellectual knowledge to practical knowledge by applying what you are learning to more and more examples from the patient's life. Technically, the patient who works in this way may be said to be (1) associating freely, (2) developing insight, and (3) working (insight) through. In the following discussion these topics are treated individually:

Associating freely—asking the basic question. Only a therapist trained in psychoanalysis should use completely free association. Other therapists should use modified free association.

One way to get the patient talking about him- or herself is by asking the following basic question as often as you can (eventually the patient will learn to ask the question of him- or herself).

The basic question is, With what in mind? This question encourages associating freely without encouraging "free association."

The patient says, "I got angry with my wife yesterday," and the therapist asks, "With what in mind?" Or the patient says, "I walked out of the drugstore with a newspaper that I stole from the rack," and the therapist asks, "With what in mind?" This question was a favorite of Dr. Sheila Hafter Gray. The question says to the patient, Tell me more—in fact tell me everything. It suggests, Let's learn together. It implies, Learning more about what you think will help you with your problems.

What is the purpose of insight?

Insight, too often beloved for itself, should always serve a purpose—to enable the patient to identify, understand, and master his problems. No purpose is served by intellectual insight without emotional insight, or with deep insight into matters of no immediate importance to the patient.

What can we expect from insight?

To misquote Santayana, understanding the past does not mean we are not condemned to repeat it. Even the best of insight often but palliates, without curing. And to be effective, insight has to be complete; partial insight may not do. To master a problem with insight, we have to understand the problem piece by piece, and unless enough pieces are understood, the insight will not help. Even with all the pieces understood, as one patient described it, "With insight I still experience my symptom, but I experience it as if through the wrong end of the telescope."

The following example illustrates (from a vignette of self-analysis) the gradual diminution of a symptom as it becomes better understood.

This patient, after receiving news that his realtor was going to sue him, developed the fear that he had left the window open in his rented office, even though he was certain that he had closed it. He analyzed this obsession on his own as a wish to hurt his landlord, a substitute for his realtor. Of course the analysis was partial (e.g., it omitted an understanding of the reason for the anger), so the obsession persisted. After continuing, "You resent the control these people have over you," the obsession became fainter; still, however, it preoccupied and worried him. Only after drawing parallels between his realtor now and his controlling, harassing father in childhood did the obsession become faint enough to seem manageable.

Of what does insight consist?

1. Making the unconscious conscious. By *insight* is often meant insight into unconscious mechanisms. This enables the patient to learn how his or her behavior is determined for, not by, him or her.

The unconscious of which we speak may be the unconscious from the past persisting into the present (the unconscious of the patient as a child or adolescent) or the newly created unconscious—daily created anew by the repression of unwanted perceptions, thoughts, and so on.

There are other aspects of insight besides making the unconscious conscious:

2. Making connections between all-conscious events of the present, until now believed disparate. This identifies complexes. For example, one patient identified an inferiority complex when she saw that "everything I do seems to be the result of the belief that I don't have what it takes." Most therapists show the patient how their complexes extend to the transference. Thus the therapist said to his patient with the inferiority complex: "You seem reluctant to get up out of the

waiting room chair and come in for your session even after I call you. I believe you are showing me that you don't feel you deserve the help that I would like to give you.''

3. Making connections between conscious past and conscious present. This shows the patient the persistent, repetitive nature of some of his or her patterns of behavior/thought. Example: "You feel I treat you now just as your mother treated you in the past." This is historical insight—important to have but not as useful as ordinarily believed.

Is there a royal road to insight?

Freud referred to the dream as the royal road to the unconscious, and so presumably to insight.

In dream interpretation, the vehicle by which we traverse this royal road, a recent event, usually from the prior day, touches upon an inactive or active complex. The patient is intellectually and emotionally moved, but the response is held back until night, when, having little else to do but sleep, he or she responds. The response is like any other response to a stimulus—a composite of the provocative event and the present active and past-but-still-active complexes. Only the form of the response is different, for at night, when we are asleep, we think more by hallucinating, something we rarely do when we are awake.

The therapist should seize upon the dream, this royal road to the unconscious, to serve his or her and the patient's purposes—the purpose of understanding. In particular, dream interpretation facilitates understanding by bypassing daytime resistances and defenses.

The following rules are suggested:

1. The therapist shall not pronounce any dreams as random and meaningless. (Although some dreams, such as the dream of running in place, somewhat like phobias of mice, seem to be both more "universal" than individual, and with less, rather than with more, personal meaning.)

2. The therapist will not assume that he or she knows what the dream means until after finding out what the patient thinks it means. Even such seemingly crystal clear dreams as overt Oedipal dreams may not mean what they seem to mean. The manifest content, in other words, is different from the latent content, or the "translation" of the dream. The therapist who translates dreams without the patient as assistant translator does so at his or her peril. Ask the patient to interpret the dream first; then add your own thoughts.

3. The therapist will ask the patient to associate to the dream. He or she may do this more than once; associations obtained even months or years after the dream are valid, revealing, and amplify the original associations.

4. The therapist will ask the patient to repeat the dream more than once. The patient often gives different versions of the dream, and it is not necessarily true that the first version is more accurate than the second, or the last.

5. The therapist will ask the patient if he or she has had the dream before.

Many dreams repeat in part or in their entirety earlier dreams, especially recurrent dreams from childhood.

In his fifties a patient had a dream that the town of Cambridge, Massachusetts, was built up with high-rise buildings. This was not much different in form and substance from a recurrent childhood dream in which he dreamed that a rustic section of a Brooklyn park was developed with skyscrapers.

6. The whole dream may be interpreted, or just parts of the interpretation may be given, other parts held back until a more appropriate time, for example, when the patient is better prepared to hear what the therapist knows.

7. The patient will not be asked to write down his or her dreams. Abraham's (1955) experience with asking the patients to write down dreams should be read and his advice heeded.

8. The patient can be taught to analyze his or her own dreams. Especially when therapy is over, the patient will have a useful tool to learn more about him- or herself. He or she can simply have a dream, then interpret it.

9. Some or all dreams should not be interpreted in some patients. For example, interpretation of dreams is likely to be too threatening for many schizophrenic patients.

Working Through

In working through, the therapist and patient repeat and revise:

1. Repetition. Breakthrough insight (eureka insight) must be repeated until fully understood, and until it thoroughly sinks in. Then it has to be extended so that it comes to explain more and more of the patient's behavior. Now each time the patient is tempted to behave in a pathological fashion, he or she thinks consciously about his or her new insight. It is hoped the insight will modify his or her response in a favorable way, for example, staying his or her hand. Eventually the new insight will become second nature, an automatic deterrent. Practice makes perfect as fixed, chronic, mindless, self-defeating, though painful, and inefficient defensive patterns—created to relieve anxiety, then maintained for secondary (as well as primary) gain—gradually yield their hold over the patient.

During the process of working through, the patient requires support in the form of assurance. Tell the patient that no matter how fixed his or her problems seem and how hopeless the task seems, the problems will likely yield to the repeated effort. A comparison with learning a foreign language may be made as an analogy to help the patient understand the eventual rewards to be expected from his or her effort.

2. Revision. Each time something new is added and something wrong is subtracted, until the patient and the therapist have a finished product.

THE END PHASE—TERMINATING

Preparing the Patient for Termination

A termination date should be set in advance so that the patient has time to discuss termination and prepare emotionally for termination.

However, some patients find the last few sessions burdensome. They run out of things to say and would just as soon terminate before the date set. Rather than insist, "No, we still have four sessions left," the therapist might allow the patient to stop earlier than scheduled.

Terminating for Positive Reasons

1. The patient feels better because the original problem has been solved, and the original problem was not a screen for or a minor problem compared with other problems.

2. The patient feels better because a little improvement in the underlying dynamic/structural problem has led to a great improvement in the presenting problem, even though the underlying problem has not been solved. Examples include significant improvement in feelings of well-being from a little reduction of guilt or from enhancement of self-esteem—not from either a flight into health or a transference cure to be followed by relapse as soon as treatment stops.

3. The patient feels better because a temporary crisis (external or internal) is over.

4. The patient feels better for any reason and wants to terminate for any reason. The therapist who counters with "After we have solved one more problem, not before" or, "What about your excessive dependency?" may be undoing months or years of good work in artificially prolonging treatment.

Terminating for Negative Reasons

1. Therapist-patient incompatibility. If a therapist, the question to ask is, this a patient you enjoy treating? and if a patient, the question is, Is this a therapist you enjoy seeing? Two people, both "good," can still have a bad relationship. Complaints about therapist "orientation" (e.g., "too behavioral," or "too analytic") are often disguised complaints about therapist style.

The therapist who takes the patient's wish to terminate as a personal slight should remember that even those patients who say they are disappointed in and have not been helped by treatment, and who quit, are often patients who can not accept what we have to offer when we are around but can accept what we have to offer after we are gone. They save their improvement for and get better (sometimes rapidly) after termination. Everything falls into place after therapy is over. The typical devaluing borderline, for example, whose splitting is manifest by him or her despising us to our face while secretly loving us behind our backs, often, on follow-up, reveals that he or she thanks us from the bottom of the heart for the help we have given, even though we are left believing that he or she hates us, finds us useless, or has been harmed.

2. Therapeutic impasse. An impasse does not mean one or both parties are malignant or incompetent. Impasses are often a matter of conflicting attitudes, preferences, or priorities. For example, the patient is free to keep his or her illness if in his or her opinion it serves a useful purpose (e.g., the relief from anxiety is worthwhile) or is not an illness but an alternative life-style. The therapist who insists, "Your being single, not married, is a sign of emotional problems," or, "You're still ill, though your schizotypal style works for you," is wrong when the patient is single out of personal preference or is odd because he or she prefers to remain odd.

Therapeutic impasses may be handled by an interruption, rather than a termination, of treatment. The therapist might say, "This is as far as we can go at this time," without a sense of finality. The therapist might say, "Wait a few months to see how you feel, then call me if you need me, and we will resume." Or the therapist might suggest a vacation from treatment. The therapist might say, "Let's take a vacation from treatment to give both of us time to think. We will resume treatment in about six months."

3. Poor results. The patient is not doing well. The patient who seems to be doing poorly may be doing poorly because of a negative or positive transference resistance (discussed in chapter 11), because something is actually wrong with treatment, or because the patient has insoluble problems. In the first case, resolve the transference resistance if possible; in the second case, change the technique if possible; and in the third, admit, to quote Jerome Weinberger (personal communication), that we are "participating in nothing," and stop. Facing reality is often refreshing and helpful for a patient who has had experience with people who distort reality, often for their own needs.

Will There Be A Relapse after Termination?

As the date for termination approaches, the patient may begin to get worse. Some patients protest termination by reviving symptoms, but they are not having a true relapse. Others are unable to handle the termination and are relapsing. How can the therapist distinguish between the two groups? A simple way is this: ask the patient. The therapist might ask, "Are you really having a relapse, or are you just frightened about being out on your own?"

What can the therapist do if the patient is becoming ill again? There are several possibilities: (1) slow down. Extend the pretermination period; (2) back off. Do not terminate. Continue as before, or continue but cut down, for example, from once a week to once every other week.

Avoiding Relapse

Some therapists anticipate and deal with the problem by avoiding it. As Dr. Daniel Dawes (personal communication) told all of his borderline patients, "You will need therapy forever. We might be able to stop for shorter or longer periods of time, but you should find a therapist and stay in that therapist's orbit for the rest of your life." He advocated continuous treatment for some of his borderline patients, intermittent treatment for others.

Intermittent treatment

There are two types of intermittent treatment. In the first, therapeutic holidays are built into the schedule of long-term therapy. A disadvantage is that treatment holidays are difficult to schedule. An advantage is that the same number of sessions can cover a greater time period; while some believe this is watering the soup—in fact, the "quiet time"—time to think and consolidate gains—between groups of sessions is often extremely helpful.

In the second, the patient is seen from crisis to crisis. One disadvantage is that crises are resolved, but there is little chance for revision of the underlying problem. But the advantages include these:

1. Patient acceptability when the patient wants only to resolve the crises. One patient, a borderline, broke up with female liaisons several times a year, each time becoming depressed. This patient wanted to continue being a borderline but did not want to have the depressions that followed the rupture of relationships.

2. Not overdoing it when crisis resolution is all that is required. Sometimes this is all that is required because between crises the patient functions normally.

3. Avoiding difficult transferences. Some borderlines, for example, do badly when caught up in an intense unmanageable transference. They have positive feelings about us when in crisis. It is after the crisis is resolved that the feelings turn negative. Such a patient sometimes is well terminated before positive turns to negative transference.

4. Avoiding rejection. Some patients, for example, borderline and depressed patients, are especially threatened by terminations (even though part of their pathology is to provoke terminations). Crisis intervention is especially appealing for these patients because it helps avoid the experience of termination.

Softening the Blow

Every patient sees termination as a rejection and a criticism, often personal. Even the patient who is told right in the beginning that the therapist is unsuitable for him or her will not believe this, secretly feeling not worthwhile. Even the patient in short-term therapy who is terminated after the agreed-on number of sessions resolutely if secretly believes, not that treatment is over, but that termination is because he or she has been a bad patient, or a bad person. And the long-term patient who resists termination does so as often out of fear of being abandoned—as a retaliation for expressed or unexpressed hostility, stubbornness, or seduction as out of pathological dependency (typically cited). The therapist who fails to analyze this component of "termination fear" will fail to undo a poisonous introject, often about to become lifelong, for his or her patient.

It certainly follows that no patient, however provocative, should be thrown out of treatment. The therapist should never tell his or her patient, "I can't continue to see you because of the way you behaved." There is always a technical reason why further treatment is not indicated, and this should be so stated as the reason for termination. In other words, the patient should not only be let down easily but also with love. Especially unacceptable is covert sadism, whereby the sadistic, hate-filled therapist keeps the reality of the termination from the patient to permit the patient to maintain and elaborate the fantasy that he or she is being thrown out.

Softening the blow of any termination when possible is telling the patient that he or she can return to treatment at any time, excepting only that the therapist may not have time to immediately see the patient even when indicated. The patient should be reassured that therapeutic time will open up (it usually does), and that he or she will be given priority listing on the waiting list. Telling the patient "come back any time" then not having the time to see the patient is one of the bad things therapists do that annoys or double binds their patients, driving them to distraction instead of curing their illness. In the few cases where no therapeutic time is available, the therapist should help the patient find another therapist.

The therapist should always make the offer to resume; the patient can always refuse it, if he or she so wishes. On the other hand, if the patient makes the offer the therapist should try not to refuse it.

Follow-ups

Try to call the patient after treatment or write to him or her to ask how he or she is doing. This provides a supportive backdrop that tells the patient, I know you are there, and you know I am there. The therapeutic process continues almost as if the therapist is still working with the patient in treatment.

Never completely sever the relationship. An example of poor technique on several levels is found in the case of the inexperienced therapist who undid years of useful work when, at the time the therapist left town, he refused to tell his patient where he was going, in the mistaken and rather inhuman belief that "this was necessary to break a possible crippling pathological continuing transference."

REFERENCES

Abraham, Karl. *Clinical Papers and Essays on Psycho-Analysis*. New York: Basic Books, 1955, vol. 2.

Bibring, Edward. The mechanism of depression. In Phyllis Greenacre (ed.), *Affective Disorders*. New York: International Universities Press, 1953.

Chapter 9

The Defense Mechanisms

Maladaptive defenses appear to the psychotherapist in at least two related forms: as resistances and as symptoms.

The therapist who successfully alters a maladaptive defense both undermines resistance to treatment and helps produce remission of symptoms.

In this chapter defense mechanism is briefly defined. Examples of resistances and symptoms derived from defense mechanisms are given. Ways to alter specific maladaptive defenses (and so resistances and symptoms) are suggested, either stated or implied.

DEFINITION OF DEFENSE MECHANISM

Analytic Model

A defense mechanism is an anxiety-reducing, thus healing, response. Its stimulus is signal, or alarm, anxiety: a warning to the ego of the possible appearance of unacceptable wishes in one's consciousness. The wishes are unacceptable because they are forbidden (guilty wishes) or overly intense (thus threatening of an intrapsychic flood).

As a classic example we might cite homosexual anxiety in a schizophrenic. The homosexual wish elicits anxiety because of guilt, and/or elicits anxiety because it threatens to overwhelm the patient, flooding him or her, perhaps causing feelings of loss of control and possible decompensation. The anxiety may be handled by the defense of projection. The patient believes, It is not I who am a homosexual; it is those around me who falsely accuse me of being homosexual. (This example is not cited to prove the origin of all paranoid delusions in unwanted homosexuality.)

Resistances to therapy appear as one manifestation of the operation of a normal or pathological defense mechanism. In the above case the patient was resistant as a result of the delusional idea, You are manipulating my mind as others are trying to manipulate my genitals. *Symptoms* are another outward manifestation of the operation of a normal or pathological defense. In the above case the patient had a paranoid delusion that "a queer, accusing angel is sitting on my shoulder," an outward manifestation of the defense of projection.

Cognitive/Behavioral Model

Conditioning and learning create and perpetuate defensiveness. For example, the individual who learns that "a good offense is the best defense" learns the defense of identifying with the aggressor; or the individual who learns to respond to a criticism with "it takes one to know one" (i.e., it is not me, it is you), has learned the defense of projection.

ALTERING THE DEFENSIVE STRUCTURE

Three Ways To Do This

1. Diminish or eliminate defensiveness.
2. Strengthen one pathological defense so that another, more pathological defense becomes unnecessary, as when strengthened repression may avoid massive regression.
3. Substitute a healthy for an unhealthy defense, for example, sublimation for regression. A defense is said to be unhealthy when it is regressive (e.g., the defense of regression); when it seriously interferes with reality testing (e.g., some denial and some projection); when it is extensive and repetitive; when it produces extensive suffering in others or in oneself; or when it is more maladaptive then adaptive.

However, to some extent, depending on its purpose, even a rigid, repetitive defense can be healthy, not pathological. An example is projection used for the healthy purpose of creating empathy (I put myself in your place to try to see how you are like me).

Some defenses seem inherently more healthy than others. For example, the defense of sublimation is a healthy defense, since it processes raw instinctual activity into refined social behavior. But even here there is latitude. For example, sublimation also has unhealthy qualities, since it renders the patient less spontaneous, less "primitive"—qualities especially admired by, and so considered healthy, in some circles.

Direct and Indirect Methods of Altering Defense

The therapist alters defenses either directly or indirectly. In the *direct* approach, the therapist might choose to suggest specific alternative, healthier defenses, for example, sublimation of anger instead of introjection of anger. In the *indirect* approach, the therapist may do the following:

1. Alter the internal economy. The therapist may diminish anxiety, and so defensiveness, by (a) diminishing the intensity of the instincts, perhaps through medication or by giving them outlet through abreaction; (b) helping the patient to feel less overwhelmed by his or her instincts through giving support; (c) diminishing guilt, for example, through identifications created by sharing experiences with those less guilty, such as the therapist.

Example. A patient described the following experience. He poured a handful of coins into the slot of a change taker on a bus. They jammed, and he could not get them moving. The bus sat still; all eyes were on him, silently demanding he disimpact the coins so that the bus could continue on its way. He felt paranoid. A woman behind him took pity and told him, "That happened to me; don't be embarrassed; and, boy (she added humorously), will you feel relief once those coins drop in." This approach (I've been through it, too; don't worry, we all have the same problem; you are not a bad person) diminished anxiety and reduced his paranoia.

2. Alter the external economy. The therapist might attempt to alter the patient's external circumstances when stressful. He or she might eliminate bad influences such as relationships or events that provoke unacceptable impulses or intolerable guilt. Or he or she might discourage behaviors that weaken the ego directly (e.g., late hours, excessive use of toxic substances), making it difficult for the patient to establish healthy defensive patterns (such as healthy repression) and promoting primitive defenses (such as unhealthy regression).

Problems Created By and Approaches To Altering the Specific Defenses

Some defense mechanisms are listed here, along with mention of some of the problems they create. In addition, some therapeutic approaches to the problems are suggested.

Sublimation

In sublimation angry and sexual feelings are bleached and converted. While the term *sublimation* is usually used to describe the conversion of undesirable instinct to desirable social behavior, the same process (with different intent) also converts undesirable instinct to undesirable social behavior. Thus the wish to harm may be sublimated into the wish to cut surgically, that is, into the wish to be a surgeon (positive sublimation); but it is often the same process that converts the wish to harm into the wish to grow rich in business, even at the expense of others (negative sublimation).

The therapist will encourage positive sublimation. But the therapist will do this cautiously, lest he or she create a patient who is all sublimation and no instinct, draining the patient of desirable hostility and sexuality and making him or her, as one patient described the outcome of his therapy, "all sweetness and light, with no emotions, and no guts."

Reaction formation

Here the patient diminishes anxiety or guilt by substituting an opposite wish or behavior. Excessiveness (going to extremes) is apparent in the outcome. While it works both ways, positive is substituted for negative (e.g., love is substituted for hate, or cooperative submission for uncooperative rebellion) more often than the other way around. This defense is especially characteristic of obsessive-compulsive patients.

The therapist might encourage socially desirable reaction formations by example, shared experiences, exhortation, and the like. Care must be taken to avoid excessiveness in the result, giving a false, inflexible, rigid quality. At other times the therapist will have not to create but to undo reaction formation, as when a patient is too kind for his or her own good, or too angry and cruel for the purposes of mastering a fear of getting too close.

Inflexible and compulsive reaction formation (covering the opposite) must be distinguished from true preference. One way of finding out if an attitude or behavior covers the opposite is this: challenge the attitude or behavior by saying, "I bet underneath you feel exactly the opposite." Care must be exercised, however, for challenging reaction formation is like opening an abdomen; it is dangerous even though usually instructive.

Repression

Perhaps distinct from suppression, a more conscious act, repression involves the dispatch of a small-to-global segment of experience, instinct, superego position, ego ideal, and so on—one that is plucked from awareness, then submerged. Because the patient is now consciously unaware of his or her feelings, they are no longer a direct source of anxiety and guilt. (When "me" is disavowed to become "not me," the defense is best called not repression but dissociation.)

Repression appears clinically in such diverse guises as an inability to perceive the true nature or consequences of one's behavior, unawareness of motivation or wish, inappropriate freedom from fear (e.g., excessive trusting), and selective or global amnesia.

The therapist may either undo or encourage repression, depending on the following:

1. The goal. Thus the therapist with a goal of social recovery for a schizo-phrenic patient will increase repression of almost everything that distracts the patient from concentrating and getting on with life. However, the therapist with the goal of analyzing a patient with a hysterical disorder may undo repression so that the patient can see how symptoms and problems in the here and now arise developmentally.

Example. A patient remembered how his adult submissiveness was attributable to his mother's reaction to his childhood defiance: she would dress him, make him pack, and make calls to the neighbors, social agencies, and so forth, looking for "a place to put you because I can't stand you any more."

Example. The patient who had recurrent dreams of low-rise towns developed with skyscrapers that were not there before developed door-checking rituals following real life achievements of which he was proud. He learned how the dreams and the symptoms could be traced to repressed childhood castration threats made by his mother when she discovered he was "playing doctor" with the girl next door.

2. The nature/structure of the symptoms. Certain symptoms (e.g., obsessions, amnesia) require the undoing of repression; while others (e.g., hallucinations) require its intensification.

3. The anticipated content of that which is repressed. For example, the un-doing of repression of forbidden homosexual wishes is usually more poten-tially devastating than the undoing of repression of forbidden heterosexual wishes.

4. The diagnosis. Repression is generally to be increased in the psychoses, otherwise generally to be decreased. There are exceptions: for example, in post-traumatic stress disorder, a nonpsychotic illness where repression might be increased because the patient is unable to forget (repress) the original trau-matic experience.

5. The patient's preference. The patient will be consulted in this matter, by being asked, "Do you want to remember, or do you want to forget?"

Isolation and displacement

1. Thought-feeling. The process of isolation and displacement of feeling has four stages (the defense we call isolation refers only to the first part, part "a," of this four-part process; the defense we call displacement refers to all four parts):

a. A feeling is isolated, or teased out, from its moorings, or connections.

b. The feeling is then removed from its moorings, or connections, and the process of transfer begun.

c. The feeling is moved elsewhere, to a new home, typically, but not nec-essarily, from a matter more to a matter less important.

d. The feeling is reattached to moorings in its new home, or berth.

Example. An obsessional patient detached his sexual feelings from women and reattached them to money. Each time he saw a desirable woman, he felt, not, I mustn't have her because it's bad to want her, but rather I can't have her because I can't afford her.

Expected consequences are viewing unimportant matters as important, or making mountains out of molehills; skewing priorities so that these unimportant matters seem to become matters of life and death; becoming depressed when that which is unimportant or merely important becomes a matter of life or death, such as, All is lost because I have dented my new car; becoming obsessive (worrisome) because of overconcern about trivial matters; and becoming phobic when the importance of the symbol (trivial prompt) replaces the importance of that which is symbolized.

A patient took out loans and dreamed of the day she would repay them. Paying off loans, important for all of us, was for her the most important thing because paying them off symbolized freedom from the poverty of her childhood. It is understandable why she became extremely depressed when ill health caused her to miss a single payment.

2. Thought-thought. The terms *isolation* and *displacement* are also used to describe thought-thought isolation and displacement—a defense characteristic of obsessive-compulsive patients who are able to worry only after failing to consider (i.e., detaching themselves from) reassuring reality. Such a patient might think of what is possible, fail to soften it by consideration of what is likely, then begin to fret and brood. Psychopaths also take thoughts out of context, but for different reasons. The psychopath, unlike the obsessional, may intend to worry, not too much, but too little. He or she then conveniently might forget to consider how his or her behavior is amoral or illegal.

3. Other displacements. The term *displacement* is also used in another way. The displacement found in projection is a displacement from within to without. Internal becomes external reality. "Me" is displaced outward to become "not me."

The therapist should undo isolation and displacement selectively, perhaps encouraging his or her patient not to treat minor matters as if they were major matters, and to pay attention to the important things in life (love, perhaps) more than the unimportant (competition, perhaps). Caution dictates that therapists not try to realign important feelings with the matters of importance to which they belong without considering negative consequences, such as the possibility of overwhelming the patient or, when reality is tragic, creating despair.

Example. A lonely elderly patient was told his preoccupation with the neatness of his apartment was a displacement from the loneliness of living by himself. Faced with his loneliness but unable to do anything about it, he killed himself.

What feelings and thoughts we realign are dependent on diagnosis. It is dangerous to dwell on anger and sexuality in paranoid patients, let alone realign these feelings willy-nilly with their source. Yet much that is useful in the treatment of paranoia may be thought of as a process of *appropriate* realignment of feelings and thoughts. Thus the therapist whose goal is to help the paranoid patient to reality test will first teach the patient that his or her incorrect perception of the world as a hostile place is a product of, and so connected to, his or her own hostility, projected outward (i.e., displaced from inward to outward), then show the patient how such feelings as intense prejudice can result from a further displacement to a detail in the persecutor's life-style.

A manic patient should always be told that his or her euphoric feelings are not only excessive but often attached to trivial matters pathologically overelaborated (e.g., one patient waxed ecstatic about his near-perfect relationship with his superintendent). Discussions of anger and sexuality forbidden in the paranoid patient can freely take place with most obsessionals, although obsessional defenses may assure that the effort fails.

Cyclic doing and undoing

(Sustained undoing may be called reaction formation.) Here the patient remains uncertain, never taking a stand, or, if taking a stand, abandoning it for its obverse. The purpose is to avoid guilt by avoiding commitment to impulses believed forbidden (while permitting a modicum of discharge).

Example. A neighbor asked a patient, "Are those mothballs any good?" The patient, afraid of assertiveness, would not answer the question. (He was afraid that a recommendation might lead to his being sued.) Instead, he answered by the noncommittal, "I have been advised that they are wise to purchase," also in this answer shifting responsibility from himself to the adviser, who could be blamed if things went wrong.

Example. Another patient told his doctor about a new subway route, then, because he feared the doctor would take the route, be mugged, and die, told him of an alternate so it would be "your choice, not mine."

Behaviorally these patients are inconsistent and unpredictable because they vacillate, usually going from one extreme to another. They seem unable to make up their mind, or, if able to do so, unable to stay with their position for very long.

Patients who cyclically do and undo are often obsessional. Obsessionals undo when they perceive their often-modest desires as immodest, their normal needs and behaviors as abnormal. They might undo normal anger with excessive kindness, and sexual feelings with protestations of lack of interest.

Though this defense relieves anxiety and guilt (by reassuring a punitive superego that anything one wishes, though bad, has been or will soon be retracted) it creates a painful perception in the patient of going crazy, and in those around him or her of being driven crazy. One patient complained, "I can't make up my mind; this makes me feel I am going crazy." The patient's wife said, "He drives me crazy by his indecision." (A positive consequence is that the therapist will have the patient and the relatives on his or her side in the quest for relief of a symptom invariably perceived to be painful.)

Treatment may be direct. Two examples, both behavioral approaches, are as follows: Encourage, advise, or exhort the patient to take a firm stand even though it means experiencing anxiety. Interrupt his or her vacillating by yelling, "Stop."

Treatment may be indirect. Two examples, the first mixed educative/analytic, the second educative, are as follows: Treat underlying guilt over success—by advice, example, and developmental review (psychoanalysis). Teach the patient what a desirable or permissible stand might be, for example, through identification with the therapist.

Regression

The regressing patient becomes defensively immature when confronted with an internal or external challenge. Since all defenses are regressive in some ways and all patients (and many normals) are defensively immature in some ways, the term *regression* might be reserved for significant immaturity, such as that found in the regressed, disorganized schizophrenic.

The therapist treating regression will use one or more of the following approaches:

1. Encouragement. Encourage the patient to grow up and stay grown (by advice, example, exhortation).

2. Relieving external pressures, where possible, such as legal difficulties, job difficulties, or difficulties with elderly parents. Self-help books and helping organizations can be of great assistance.

Hospitalization, while it in some ways promotes regression, can also diminish it by removing the patient from a regression-provoking environment.

3. Resolving internal conflicts that characteristically encourage, promote, or cause regression, as with those sexual conflicts that tempt the patient to become "regressively asexual," or those conflicts over independence that promote regressive dependency.

Example. A patient in his 60s had no sexual relationships of any kind for over 20 years. Though desirous of "getting in a car and taking an automobile trip with a woman—that would give me the most pleasure of all," he in fact limited himself to such joys as the joy of saving money and the joy of honing and refining his relationship with his elderly mother.

The patient was informed that success was not forbidden, encouraged not to allow his sense of guilt to continue to forbid him the pleasure of a relationship with a woman, and reassured that having a relationship with a woman was compatible with a continuing relationship with his mother—it was not, as he believed, one or the other. He was advised to exchange his low-dividend-paying stocks for high-dividend-paying bonds so that he might have more income to use for dates with women. He was directed to groups where others might push him and where he might meet friends or eligible partners.

The patient also illustrates how regression due to unavoidable external circumstances seems irreversible while the circumstances remain unchanged: this patient responded only weakly to treatment improving the most when his elderly mother died.

To be distinguished from pathological regression is regression in the service of the ego—a temporary, pleasurable, productive, healing regression, such as a vacation.

Denial

This defense is prominent in patients with a manic/hypomanic affective disorder. The euphoric mood may result either from a denial of depression or a denial of the thoughts and feelings that give rise to the depression.

Some clinicians reserve the term *denial* for alterations of perception of internal reality (feeling and thought), while others also use the term for alterations of perception of external reality. An example of denial of internal reality is, I deny that I am a bad person with mean thoughts; in fact, I am a saint. One patient, confronted with how she created her own difficulties with others, disagreed, saying, "My only problem is that I don't have any problems; my only evil is that I am too good." An example of denial of external reality is, She didn't die; I know she lives.

Sometimes it is difficult to tell what is external and what internal; for example, it is difficult to tell if denial of illness is a denial of either internal or external reality, or both. An example of denial of both internal and external reality is the manic denial of identity in a patient whose identity was that of failure. While being interviewed on hospital rounds, she ran to the front of the room, faced her audience as if an actress, pirouetted, sang and whistled a popular song, then bellowed with false pride, "And then I wrote . . . "

Denial is a defense that supports other defensive operations. Denial typically supports the defense of repression (1) by working with it toward the shared goal of alteration of one's perception of internal reality and (2) by appearing in its place when repressed material returns spontaneously or is recovered through therapy. (This, not the joy of learning, may be what we see when an on-target clarification or interpretation is accompanied with, or followed by, transient euphoria.)

Denial productive of immediate or potential psychological or real harm *must* be challenged. One respectful technique adaptable to challenging denial, especially in the more paranoid denying patient, is that of Frieda Fromm-Reichmann (1960, 175) who (in another context) advised against arguing with the patient, stating instead that there are differences of interpretation, and recommending an investigation into the reasons why the patient and the psychiatrist do not see and hear the same thing. Other patients, those less paranoid, may be approached more directly. They may be told, "You are denying," and further told, "It is better for you to face what you are denying."

Some of the same cautions in challenging projection and paranoia are applicable to challenging denial. Care must be taken to challenge, not condemn. The possibility that the patient is right must be considered (the patient denying death may in fact not be dying). And the patient must be allowed to maintain as much self-respect and self-esteem as possible throughout.

In some ways the treatment approach for denial and the consequences of denial are not the same as, but the opposite of, the treatment approach used for most other patients, for example, the obsessive-compulsive or the hysteric. The patient should be told, not, "You are more worried than you need to be," but, "You aren't worried enough." The denying patient, unlike the obsessive-compulsive or the hysteric, should not be encouraged to be happy. Instead, he or she should be told, "Your happiness is inappropriate, and you should look for reasons to worry." The therapist may also have to increase, not decrease, guilt and anxiety.

Caution: Even though the denial is pathological, do not disrupt fantasies in patients who need them. The lonely patient should be allowed to keep the solace of an overdone-in-fantasy relationship needed to sustained him or her through a period of isolation, and in cases of terminal illness, denial might be encouraged and supported, not removed.

Introjection/internalization/identification

These defenses are primarily geared to handle anger. (One cannot with much reason speak of introjection of sexuality.)

1. Introjection. By *introjection* is meant this: anger that is directed toward another instead of (a) being expressed outwardly is (b) expressed inwardly. The result is that the anger is expressed at oneself, instead of at the other person.

2. Internalization. By *internalization* is meant this: the anger, because of being kept inside, becomes an internal, not external, anger.

3. Identification. By *identification* is meant this: we become like the object of our anger. Identification results from introjection and internalization, as follows. It results because the inevitable consequence of keeping anger with another in, and taking anger with another out on, oneself is that the patient treats him- or herself just like the person who originally provoked the anger. If "I am mad at you" becomes "I am mad at me," by extension, "you" and "me" are now rather alike. (This is secondary identification. Primary identification is an almost opposite process in which, through empathy, we position ourselves to be like another often *in order to* avoid expressing anger. For example, we think, I become like you, and try to guess what you are thinking and feeling, so that I can avoid getting angry with you.)

It is worth noting that because the capacity to identify depends on the capacity to differentiate oneself from others, if only then to blur the differentiation, the capacity to identify implies a degree of differentiation, that is, of developmental maturity. For this reason the capacity for identification may not exist in primitive, immature, undifferentiated narcissistic and schizophrenic patients, who have a blurring of identity resulting from an inability to distinguish themselves from other people.

Hint: Though the introjection of anger may be said to be a cause of depression, getting anger out may worsen not relieve depression. Expressing anger can increase guilt (guilt is one reason for depression) and scare the patient who believes, My anger will drive everyone away. In part for this reason, some therapists find that in treating depression it is better to let anger express itself. This can occur (a) once guilt is diminished and (b) the patient is helped either to feel more certain of the stability of his or her relationships or feel more certain of his or her capacity to do without should there be a loss.

Projection

In projection, both as a normal or pathological mechanism, we attribute our own feelings, impulses, wishes, and so on, to a source in the external world. The results of projection include the following:

1. A distortion of one's perception of external reality (since it becomes commingled with internal reality).

2. A tendency to feel persecuted. One's unwanted impulses will soon victimize one, not from within, but from without. Typically, a hostile patient becomes the object of his or her own forbidden angry desires, now reposing in another person.

3. A tendency to feel anger toward another, instead of feeling guilt about one's unacceptable anger. This is the mechanism: after transferring or displacing anger to others, the patient angrily criticizes others for being angry at him or her.

4. A tendency to feel seduced (erotomania, really erotoparanoia) as one becomes the object of one's own forbidden erotic desires, now reposing in another person.

The cautious therapist will be gentle in challenges to projection, challenging the patient's view of reality and the people in it cautiously, with understanding and compassion and without implying that the patient is crazy, though psychotic he or she may (or may not) be. Otherwise the therapist provokes excessive anxiety and guilt. The anxious/guilty patient may now incorporate the therapist into his or her delusional system. For example, the patient may think, I am not angry; my problem is that you pick on me. The therapist, now the enemy, is condemned, sued, attacked, or murdered, first as the bearer of the patient's forbidden wishes, second as the person responsible for having called them to the patient's attention.

REFERENCE

Fromm-Reichmann, Frieda. *Principles of Intensive Psychotherapy*. Chicago: The University of Chicago Press, 1960.

Chapter 10

Miscellaneous Matters

Therapists tend to be unthinking about the following:

1. Determining the length of treatment and frequency of sessions. Examples: One therapist saw all patients for as long as they wanted to be in treatment. Another saw all patients twice a week because, "Once-a-week sessions were too far apart." A third, a pharmacotherapist, saw most patients once a month because "thirty-day prescriptions are the most convenient to write."

2. Structuring the setting for treatment. This includes such housekeeping matters as the physical appearance of the office.

3. Therapist and patient behaviors before, after, or in-between treatment sessions. This includes waiting room conduct, conduct when the therapist and patient meet outside the session, and phone calls and emergencies between sessions.

In this chapter we discuss ways to handle some of these miscellaneous matters. Because our goal is to encourage a healthy obsessionalism, the chapter's structure follows tripartite division of the obsessive-compulsive personality into concerns with time, money, and orderliness (organizational matters).

TIME

How Long Should I Treat?

Try not to have a one-size-fits-all attitude toward the length of treatment and frequency of sessions. Try not to think, All patients should be seen for a total of 12 sessions, or, All patients should be seen for a lifetime.

The single consultation

Never minimize the potential good that can come from a single consultation, either a consultation with a patient not presently in treatment or a consultation with a patient presently in treatment with another therapist.

Example. A patient in analysis sought consultation because he was "depressed because I am not getting along well with my analyst." This patient's depression improved when he was told that, in the consultant's opinion, it was not he who was hypersensitive but his analyst who, for reasons of his own, was too hypercritical.

Especially desirable is a two-session consultation with a week between sessions. This gives the therapist time to "sleep on it," to think about, revise, and refine his or her thoughts about the patient in the period between the two sessions. Two sessions also reduce pressure on the therapist to respond immediately, perhaps impulsively.

Short-term therapy

This is also discussed in chapter 7. Indications for short-term therapy include the following:
1. A crisis. The crisis may be either real (traumatic in origin) or fantasied. An example of a real, traumatic crisis is the case of the patient, presented in chapter 7, who entered an appliance store and was trapped by a gunman who took hostages, shooting several.
An example of a crisis in fantasy is the following:

A patient said, "I am in crisis because I bought a second house before I sold the first and now cannot sell the first." The crisis was less real than it appeared because it was virtually certain that the first house would sell, given enough time. The real crisis was due to the patient's sense of personal rejection that appeared whenever a potential buyer decided not to buy.

2. A maturational symptom. An example is Elizabeth Zetzel's case (also mentioned in chapter 5) of the young man who developed an acute bridge phobia when about to marry a woman who lived on the other side of a bridge. Another example is the patient who, when about to marry, developed diffuse somatic preoccupations, especially complaints about her feet. She could not be properly fitted for wedding shoes "because of bunions" and put off the wedding date to have what she called "emergency corrective surgery."
3. A nonmaturational illness, encapsulated, with uncomplicated Oedipal dynamics. (Developmentally earlier problems—in analytic terminology, anal and oral problems—are often too invasive, deep-rooted, and primitive, nonverbal, to so easily yield).
4. A self-limited illness that has a self-limited course (including schizophreniform disorder and acute depressions) or is cyclical (e.g., a bipolar disorder).

Long-term therapy

By *long term* is meant months to years. Different reasons that patients might require long-term treatment are the following:

1. The illness is chronic and severe. Sometimes it seems as if one year of therapy is required to undo one year of psychological damage.

2. The illness is complex, overdetermined.

One patient required 25 years of therapy so that a capacity to love maturely might emerge from Oedipal fixation and obsessional guilt. The favorable result appeared only after a combination of therapist urging, permission giving, analysis of Oedipal fears, analysis of fear of being controlled, and analysis of fear of merging and loss of identity. (Also helpful was the presence of a "newly born" therapist who, able to work out her own similar problems, also after 25 years, was able to provide her patient with the healthy model she needed!)

3. Crises are recurrent, either because they are self-generated or because of repeated bad luck. Treatment may be a holding operation through crises (e.g., treatment of some psychopathy consists of keeping the patient out of trouble or getting the patient out of trouble once in) or until remission (e.g., some personality disorders have to be "held" for 20 or so years until they remit, characteristically in middle age).

4. Comprehension is slow. This may be due to low intelligence, lack of psychological sophistication, or extreme resistance.

5. Possibility of deterioration. Patients who improve only sightly with treatment might have gotten a great deal worse without it.

How Often Should We Have Our Sessions?

Do not scoff at therapy that is less than once a week. It is not only for the patient who is being monitored for drug effect. We can educate, even interpret, with once- or twice-a-month therapy. It can work extremely well. It works for the schizoid or elderly patient who finds that once or twice a month is enough to provide a healing sense of companionship. It works for the obsessional who finds that the sense of informality given by the wide spaces between sessions helps him to or her relax about the treatment. It works when occasional—but not on that account, less effective—reminders suffice: for schizotypal patients told that salvation may lie in either rejoining the society in which they find themselves or in moving to a place where they are better accepted, for depressed patients told they are not the bad person they believe themselves to be, and for psychopathic/antisocial patients told their misbehavior is counterproductive, self-defeating, intolerable, dangerous, and/or unlawful. There are even advantages.

It is cheaper. It takes up less time. Countertransference and transference problems may be minimized or altogether avoided. And we do not find ourselves repeating ourselves because we have run out of new things to say.

Frequency as related to diagnosis

Determination of frequency of sessions is partly a function of diagnosis. The dependent patient and the depressed patient may predictably find that once-a-week therapy sessions are spaced too far apart for comfort, while the paranoid patient may predictably find that twice-a-week therapy is too intense. Some paranoid patients are predictably convinced that the therapist who sees them more than once a week sees them more than needed for the money, no matter what we say to the contrary.

Of course, diagnosis is not the only determinant of frequency. As a simple example, three times a week may be too intense for the patient who is not sure whether or not to abandon his or her personality disorder, but not enough for the patient with the same personality disorder who finds it a burden and can wait to get rid of it.

MONEY

Setting the Fee

On patients asking the fee

Some patients ask your fee for different reasons. Some ask the fee because it is entirely sensible to know how much therapy costs. Some ask the fee because they are comparison shopping. This may be because they are frugal or because they cannot afford too high a fee. Still others ask the fee for pathological reasons, often diagnosis dependent. Obsessive-compulsive patients want to know the fee because it gives them a sense of completeness from which may then come a sense of control. Or, if they are planning to withhold payment, they want to know how much they are going to be withholding. One obsessional with masochistic features unconsciously wanted to know the fee so that he could bounce a check, feel guilty, then suffer as he made reparations. Dependent patients may, though wealthy, want to reassure themselves that they will not run out of money and lose the relationship. Finally, a few patients—the more sadistic and/or psychopathic—want to know the fee because they want to know how much they are never going to pay.

Still other patients do not seem to want to know what therapy costs. This is reasonable when they are wealthy enough so that it does not matter. At other times it is for pathological reasons, often diagnosis dependent. If dependent, they might assume that even if they cannot afford the sessions, they will get them anyway. Or, if hypomanic, they might assume they can afford them even when they cannot.

Because it is impossible for the therapist to know the patient's dynamics, the therapist should follow his or her own procedure, even though it might not be the one best tailored for the patient.

On therapists telling the patients the fee

Some therapists prefer to tell the patient the fee at the beginning. Such a therapist might say, over the phone, "My fee is so-and-so per session, or thus for the first session, thus for subsequent sessions." (Sometimes the therapist charges the same fee for the first and subsequent sessions, sometimes an initial consultation is more than subsequent consultation/therapy sessions.) Some therapists tell the patient they do not charge for a first session if there is no second session. Two advantages for this practice are generating good will and often being able to set a fairer fee if you postpone fee discussion until the first session (when you can learn more about your patient's needs).

Tell the patient if you expect payment on a per-session basis or prefer to bill and do not mind waiting.

The therapists who prefer to discuss fees after the first contact, not before, should be prepared to adjust the fee for the first session if the patient is displeased with the fee or believes that an initial contact without a promise of subsequent treatment is a contact not worth being reimbursed. Particular effort should be devoted to not double bind the patient—by telling the patient that that you set a fee only after you see him or her, then setting a fee the patient cannot afford, complaining when he or she protests and insisting that payment be made for a session of whose cost there was no advance knowledge and is not affordable.

In these matters the therapist's policy often depends on the population being treated. A therapist in a big city working with low-paid theater people might have some policies that differ from a therapist in a wealthy suburb working with high-paid well-insured executives.

Raising and Lowering the Fee

Therapists usually adjust their fees for new patients to keep up with inflation. It is not always necessary to raise the fee in round numbers. Sheila Hafter Gray raised the fee in accordance with the inflation index, making for such complex numbers as $73.89 a session—numbers that seemed, but were not, fatuous. Therapists who raise fees because of inflation should consider lowering them because of recession.

Some therapists treating patients long term suggest raising the fee for a patient already in treatment for the following reasons: because of inflation, when the patient's financial circumstances improve independently, and when the patient's financial circumstances improve as the result of treatment—so that the therapist as well as the patient can benefit financially from side effects of good psychological health. Dr. Gray suggests that the initial therapeutic contract with long-term patients, for example patients with a personality disorder, include a clause describing policies about raising fees during treatment.

To be consistent, the therapist should lower the fee for the following reasons: during a recession, when the patient suffers financial reverses, and when the patient is unable to afford as much because of psychological deterioration (unless stemming from acting-out, in which case the patient would be asked to continue to pay the full fee, if possible, so that the therapist is not the victim of the acting out.)

Different Fees for Different Patients?

There are times when sliding scales are illegal (for example with some contractual arrangements).

Nonverbal Meaning of the Fee

The fee says something to the patient about the therapist. Some therapists increase their stature in the eyes of the patient by charging high fees, the patient believing, If my therapist is this expensive, he or she must be good. Conversely, some therapists lower their stature in the eyes of the patient by keeping their fee low. Finally, all of this can, like any manipulation, backfire, for example, when the shrewd patient learns how, more often than not, fees have no relationship to competency. (One patient did research and discovered that some good therapists charged low fees because they were compensated by academia, some because they were compensated by royalties from books they had published, some because they had institutionally regulated fees, and some because they were independently wealthy.)

To compete, a therapist may either lower the fee (so that people can better afford to come to him or her) or raise his or her fee (so that his or her patients feel he or she is one of the best).

ORDERLINESS (ORGANIZATION)

Sound and Acoustics

Keep sound from traveling from the office to the waiting room. The patient in the office is entitled to privacy, and should not have his or her private affairs overheard by a stranger, a potential rival (as in some training sessions), or, as happened in one case, by an enemy. The next patient is predictably threatened and upset by being able to overhear, and often too polite to complain. Double doors made of solid wood and stripped around the perimeter are a necessity. A sleep-sound machine suppresses most sound emanating from the office and is not annoying to the patient in the waiting room. An FM radio in the waiting room blocks sound from the office but interferes with the patient's ability to think, do pretherapeutic work, or, a habit of some obsessionals, prepare the session to come. Sometimes the patient who does not like the station turns the sound down or turns the radio off, and your protection is gone.

Comfort

As Freud said, one should treat the patient like an invited guest. He or she will always appreciate comforts and necessities such as tissues, a place to put boots, umbrella and coat, and so forth. Some patient too polite to complain, will if mistreated retaliate in passive-aggressive fashion by bridling with controlled angry behavior that looks characterological but is in some respects actually realistic, human, and expected. In most cases an uncomfortable or inappropriately decorated office is provocative enough to emphasize an aspect of the patient's problem that was otherwise insignificant, giving the wrong diagnostic impression.

Appearance of the Office

Though you live in your office, do not bring much, if anything, about your personal life into it. Such necessities as a coffee maker are permissible. Diplomas, books, and, if analytically oriented, a picture of Freud, are also allowed. But such things as hunting trophies and pictures of wife and children are unwise to display. Hide personal items such as your camera equipment or your shopping. Items of borderline acceptability include those that are somewhat frightening, such as primitive masks with a feral look; abrasive, such as some abstract paintings; and incongruous, such as pictures of Freud rendered ironic by a therapist's drug or behavioral orientation.

Arranging Yourself with the Patient

Face to face or couch?

Face-to-face treatment provides some of the same satisfactions as a real relationship and so can substitute, in part, for a real relationship. For example, it can fill a void for the lonely, isolated patient, and counteract withdrawal and dereism in autistic patients.

Because of its quality of being real, this treatment can be a vehicle for influencing the patient directly—through advice, suggestion, or manipulation.

Put the patient on a couch, and some of these benefits are lost. The therapist becomes remote and disembodied. The patient's fantasy grows, and the autistic paranoid or grandiose individual becomes more autistic, and more delusional. Schizoid patients who are already on a couch in their own lives and not facing other people in the way they should, borderlines with a tenuous hold on reality, and obsessionals who depend on close observation of minutiae to ward off anxiety may also suffer. The couch, as Dr. Grace DeBell said (personal communication), is a dangerous instrument. Never, never use it unless you have had special training.

Of course, the couch can be a useful instrument as well. Treatment on the couch promotes fantasy buildup. The therapist becomes a screen, a pure transference figure. The patient, ever amazing him- or herself, uses the transference to learn about what is going on inside. And the comfortable therapist, not having to be stared at or to control his or her nonverbal responses, can think and respond without distraction.

Using a desk and chair or two chairs?

Some therapists who do face to face prefer to sit behind a desk. It helps some maintain distance from their patients. It helps others differentiate themselves from their patients. Some patients prefer the therapist behind a desk for the same reasons. Other therapists and patients find this arrangement too distant and inhuman and prefer face to face using two chairs. Here the chairs should be comfortable, and the same kind of chair might well be used for both patient and therapist. Some therapists sit in different places with different patients. One therapist sat behind a desk for paranoid patients who needed distance and sat face to face with schizoid patients who did not do well when the therapist removed himself behind a desk. Practically speaking, the therapist usually prefers to work only one way and is unable to adjust to the patient's needs.

Dress code

The therapist's dress must be comfortable. A suit and tie, if uncomfortable, are not necessary.

The therapist must, if he or she wears tags of national origin, be attentive to the patient's inevitable response. Never act as if you are not wearing a yarmulke or a sari. Always ask the patient about his or her reaction and expect there will be one. The response may be appropriate (interest, for example) or inappropriate. Xenophobic paranoid patients typically react with anxiety to foreign touches in a therapist's appearance. Some patients, more positively but just as inappropriately, find these touches reassuring. For example, they might reassure the anxious Oedipal patient that this is "clearly not my parent." (The same is applicable for therapists who are racially defined.)

Taking notes

Taking notes is a good thing to do because it is the only way to record material verbatim. Wait until the end of the session and you will leave something out, alter the production, and so forth. Try to develop the technique of writing automatically, so that you do not lose rapport with the patient.

Allow the patient to eat during sessions?

Cold soda, especially on a hot day, or hot coffee, especially on a cold day, are permissible, since these make the patient comfortable, do not interfere with talking, and are not necessarily adopted for hostile purposes. On the other hand, the patient who chews gum throughout is impossible to talk to, and the patient who eats is often not hungry but more often acting in, possibly behaving so as to reproduce a family scene by eating together, possibly being hostile by dropping crumbs to sully the office.

The bathrooms

Separate bathrooms, if possible, are best. If not, the therapist will simply have to admit the facts of life and on occasion use the bathroom with the patient in the waiting room—waiting and watching. In such instances the therapist will have to be careful to lock the door after entering and adjust his or her clothing before leaving. It is not only the patient's problem when, for example, the patient assumes that a therapist, who emerges with unzipped pants or skirt that remain that way during the session is fair game either for seduction or condemnation, or both. (In one case a suspicious paranoid patient failed to recover from an entire session that was held with the therapist's pants zipper open—a session that may in fact have been instrumental in her eventual suicide.) Always wash your hands. The patient who does not hear the water running may be right to complain about the therapist's unsanitary behavior.

OTHER

Other neglected matters deserving of care and attention are as follows.

Number of Therapists

One, two, or more therapists?

Should a patient have only one therapist? Why not two, sequentially or simultaneously? Is individual treatment with a psychiatrist combined with group therapy with a psychologist, or individual treatment with a psychologist or social worker combined with pharmacotherapy by a psychiatrist, in some ways even superior to treatment with one therapist? Should we apply the proverb, Too many cooks . . . or the proverb, Two heads . . . ?

1. Sequentially. Some patients should return to the same therapist each time they need treatment. One patient did well selecting an analytically oriented therapist, another a behaviorally oriented therapist, for each period of treatment. Others may learn from one therapist, then go on to learn even more, or something different, from another therapist. In one case the patient did well each time selecting a therapist of a different persuasion, the new supplementing and reinforcing the old, dynamic knowledge supplementing and reinforcing behavioral and cognitive approaches. In other cases when the old therapy is flawed, the new therapy can undo some of the damage.

A patient in analysis for a characterological depression complained that the man in the apartment above was banging on his ceiling to get the patient to stop using his air conditioner. The analyst replied, "You can't tolerate the banging because it reminds you of your father who used to bother and annoy you in the middle of the night." When the patient hired a lawyer to stop the banging, the analyst suggested, "This is your way of getting back at your father—a symbolic castration." The patient became more depressed, felt more helpless, and believed, If I were a good person, she would help me have a quiet apartment, not criticize me for complaining about the noise, then castrate me when I try to get help. The patient acted out by moving to another city to punish his analyst for her failure of empathy.

Many years later the patient returned for therapy. The depressive cloud from the last analysis still hanging over his head, he told his new therapist the story of the air conditioner. The therapist inquired, "Yes, but what were you to do about the banging? The original formulation traced the roots of a problem but overlooked its practical, here and now, significance. So it went nowhere and understandably created bad feelings in you. Looks as if the implied criticism stayed with you as a poisonous introject." The poisonous introject was thereby removed, and the resultant depressive cloud finally, after many years, lifted.

2. Simultaneously. This can be effective so long as neither of the parties is mean spirited. It does not work when simultaneous treatment of the same patient is the occasion for working out rivalries between schools, professions, people. In one case a husband and wife were being seen by two therapists. The husband's therapist, believing the wife's therapist was prescribing too many drugs, took every opportunity to speak ill of the wife's therapist. This backfired: first it inspired the husband to defend his wife's therapist from attack; then it inspired the husband to quit therapy with "anybody who would bad-mouth another person this way." Eventually the husband joined the wife in couple therapy, where he could help his wife directly by joining the wife and her therapist in a bitter counterattack.

Simultaneous pharmacotherapy and psychotherapy

The question is often asked, How do I treat a patient in psychotherapy when he or she is receiving psychoactive drugs? Though believed to be a hard question to answer, it is actually easy. If the patient is receiving the correct medication, then whatever symptoms can be treated with drugs are being so treated. It is the problems that *remain* that, presumably insensitive to drugs, require treatment with a form of psychotherapy. In other words, treat what remains to be treated. (To minimize patient confusion, the patient seen by a nonmedical therapist for therapy and a psychiatrist for drugs should have as little conflicting psychotherapy from the psychiatrist as possible.)

Starting Up

Tell the patient to wait in the waiting room until it is time for the session. Tell the patient you will appear when it is time. When it is time open the doors (the double doors to block sound from the office!), smile, and say hello. Hello is all the therapist says at this moment. Prolonged conversations about the weather or about other trivialities are to be avoided. Especially to be avoided is a conversation in which the therapist asks, "How are you?" obviously hoping to hear, "Fine," followed by, "Nice day, isn't it?" Therapy is meaningful, and this is meaningless. First, the patient would not be there if he or she were fine. Second, you may find yourself in the position of talking about the weather in the waiting room with a patient who is about to confess suicidal fantasies when he or she gets into the office. Third, anything said at this time will influence the course of the session. The danger is that the patient will associate to one of the therapist's (trivial) productions, not to one (meaningful) of his or her own.

You should interrupt should the patient begin to talk about problems when still in the waiting room. Ask the patient to wait until he or she is seated in the office. The therapist might say, "Why not come into the office, have a seat, then we will proceed. What you have to say is too important for the waiting room."

Now lead the patient to the office doors, permitting the patient to enter before you. The therapist then shuts the doors after the patient. You are the therapist, it is your office, and you should keep control of the doors. Particular care needs to be taken that female therapists avoid permitting a male patient to hold the doors open for them. This of course encourages identity (who is treating whom?) and role (who is in charge?) confusion and suggests a subordinate position for women.

Wait for the patient to talk first, and look eager to hear what the patient has to say. Bringing up a topic of your own to start the session is often not wise. Perhaps the patient has spent days between sessions thinking about how to start the session. Perhaps the patient has something very momentous, serious, and even tragic to say that you will interrupt with something trivial that has importance only for you. Do not say anything even when you have agreed to continue a discussion from the last session. By now the topic still important in your mind may be unimportant for the patient.

While the initial words should ideally come from the patient, sometimes the patient has trouble talking. In the first session this is often not because of resistance but because of a lack of schooling or experience in the technique of talking to a therapist. While watching the patient struggle can be educational—for in this way we can learn about diagnosis and dynamics—much more is to be gained by bypassing the problem to get on with the session. So you might make an opening sound (such as, "So?" or "Yes?"), make a general opening statement ("I'm all ears"), ask a general question, such as, "What's bothering you?" or use the silence as an occasion to restate a version of the basic rule. Sometimes you have to guess the diagnosis and intervene accordingly. If you guess the patient is silent because he or she is paranoid, reassure the patient that the material is confidential, that you are not an adversary, and so on. Or, if you guess the patient is silent because he or she is obsessional, tell the patient which topic might be a good one to start the session.

Ending

Do not continually follow the passage of time with a watch. The patient will notice each time you look at your wrist and think, You can't wait until the time is up, can you? Instead, use a clock placed where you can comfortably see it, without squinting or craning your neck.

When the time is up, act swiftly and firmly. This is not the moment for guilt about how much you are charging and how little the patient is getting. Say, "We have to interrupt for now; our time is up." This has the advantage of giving the patient the reason for the interruption. This way he or she does not believe the interruption to be for another reason, for example, because the patient has said something the therapist disapproves of. If the topic being discussed warrants further discussion, the therapist might say, "Though we have to interrupt for now, we can (or should) continue discussing that next week."

Some patients will hesitate to, be unable to, or refuse to end the session. Among these patients are ambivalent schizophrenic patients who are inspired to begin just when you are inspired to end, paranoid patients who think you are shorting their time, and dependent patients who are too anxious to leave.

Many resistant patients save the best for last—so they might present it when it is too late for complete discussion and therapist response. If possible, the therapist should tell the patient that because it is important, this material will have to wait for the body of a session so that it can be dealt with thoroughly, not on the fly.

The end of the session presents special problems for obsessive-compulsive patients. Many perceive the beginning and end of the session to represent a kind of control. They deal with feeling controlled by being stubborn and oppositional. They withhold until the last moment, then, sensing the session is over, open up. Now they are controlling you! Also, anxious because they feel they wasted the session, they try to get it all out before it is too late. Some accomplish the same end (and retaliate for your ending the session) by choosing the end of the session to brood, perhaps about a matter not easily resolved. One patient compared his end-of-the-session behavior to his hand-washing compulsion, geared to keeping him and members of his household from leaving for an outside activity.

Obsessive-compulsive patients sometimes knock on the door after the session and come back, either to talk about something they forgot to say or to repeat a worry once or a few more times before finally going. The patient with the clean cup ritual returned after he had left the office. The lights were off, and the therapist was about to leave when the buzzer rang. The patient returned to throw away the used cup he left in the bathroom because he was afraid others would use it and get a disease. The kind, patient therapist will expect the knock on the door, expect the patient back, and either leave time for this ritual or give the patient a little extra time when he or she appears. Fortunately, only the severely ill patient will persist; most patients will recognize that they are doing something insupportable and cease and desist after a short period of time. During the interchange the therapist should smile, nod his or her head politely, and repeat over and over, "We best discuss this, your problem, next time," or, "But we do have to interrupt for now." You might also say to the patient that he or she is acting ill, and/or acting in, and that learning how to stop the session on time, not prolong it, is part of the cure. Try telling the patient that stopping on time is more helpful than harmful because he or she probably wants to be controlled, and because if given too much more time, feels guilty. If in a rush, try telling the patient the truth—that you have a schedule to keep. But, whatever you do, do not start up psychotherapeutic discussion again.

This said, we have to recognize that some of these patients try us sorely and get under our skin. Even the best of us becomes impatient, angry, or "gets the creeps" because the person before us is coming back over and over to repeat something again and again as if possessed. (One patient on an in-patient service drove the staff to distraction by coming back over and over to ask, "Did I bump you?" Sometimes when he came back to ask, he in fact bumped into a staff member, thereby creating a reason for him to come back again to ask, "Did I bump you?") Finally, we have to face how coming back again and again after the session is over may mean the patient is too ill to be treatable with psychotherapy alone.

Always recognize holidays or special occasions. Wish the patient a Merry Christmas or a Happy Birthday. But never wish the depressed patient, "Have a nice day." This will certainly plunge the patient into intensified gloom, in part because he or she will leave thinking, My therapist doesn't understand me. Say, instead, "I hope you will soon improve enough so that I can wish you a nice day."

Finally, do not say anything mysterious that might worry the patient for a week. Either the patient will call you up to find out what you meant or suffer worrying about it until the next session. The therapist who smiles knowingly and says, "Next time we should discuss where your therapy is going," is carelessly unempathic or carefully hostile.

Phone Calls

Though some therapists believe the patient is guilty until proved innocent, and assume all phone calls are symptomatic, resistant, and/or acting out, in fact there are at least four reasons that a patient might call:

1. To schedule or reschedule an appointment. They have to schedule or reschedule an appointment because something unanticipated, though nonemergent, has come up—for example, a business meeting. The healthier the patient, the more involved, the more times he or she will have to reschedule appointments for this reason. When there are both real and psychological reasons for the

requested change, the patient should be given the benefit of the doubt unless changing appointments becomes habitual. Sometimes it is difficult to tell what exactly is the patient's motivation, as when a patient waits too long to call. Thus one patient who could have reasonably been expected to anticipate worsening snow conditions called to cancel after the session started. He said that "he was waiting for a break in the snow storm right up to the time of his session, but there was none, so he has decided to stay home."

2. There is a legitimate emergency. What is a "legitimate" emergency? Some therapists define an emergency as follows: If the patient feels it is an emergency, then it is an emergency. Not the patient's plight, but his or her reaction to it, his or her belief about its seriousness and urgency, is considered the deciding factor. Other therapists define an emergency, not by the patient's assessment of his or her plight, but by the plight itself. Such therapists believe that some plights are inherently greater than others and can be graded into emergent and nonemergent. Because both are right, the definition of what is and what is not an emergency is a personal one, often a matter of conscience. The purist is correct in his or her belief that the "emergency response" can, like any other response, be analyzed, and that responding to the reality ("All of us would become anxious") detracts from the therapist's ability to analyze it ("You become anxious because of a childhood fixation"). But the patient who admires the therapist for his or her theoretical prescience will secretly damn the therapist for an uncaring, unfeeling attitude—even though it may in a good intellectual cause. For this reason it is best to believe the patient, sympathize, handle the emergency, then analyze it later (if at all).

In the beginning, emergencies may be created to test the therapist. The patient might have one emergency to reassure him- or herself that the therapist is there "in case," and once reassured, never have another. That said, emergencies should be anticipated and avoided as much as possible. Too many phone calls may mean that the patient requires another session or sessions, to be scheduled first on an emergency, then on a regular, basis. The patient's failure to avoid, or need to create, emergencies, as well as the content of the emergency are potentially analyzable. Finally, while patients should be reminded that avoiding anxiety (and so emergencies) is a high priority activity, others who are being helped to *increase* anxiety (e.g., the schizoid patient who uses isolation to avoid healthy interpersonal anxiety) might be congratulated, not treated, for an emergency, while being reminded, maintaining one's sense of humor, that perhaps they have done too well becoming involved.

Rule: All emergencies that are reactive—that follow sudden, unexpected, and unavoidable tragedies, whether minor (a critical letter) or major (a death)— should be taken seriously. The likelihood that the patient is behaving neurotically, acting out, and/or resisting decreases when there is a sudden, adverse change in the patient's circumstances.

Suicidal talk, threats, or activity is *always* an emergency. The therapist should ask such questions of *cause* as, "Do you feel depressed?" "Are voices telling you to do it?'' ''Are you doing it because you feel paranoid?'' Questions of *intent* should be asked, such as, ''Do you plan to do it?'' ''What exactly do you plan to do?'' *Historical* questions should be asked, such as, ''Have you tried to do it before?'' ''Is there a family history?'' *Commonsense* questions should be asked, such as, ''What would you like me to do to help?'' (Remember, the patient is not necessarily calling to bother, bedevil, or attack you with his or her suicidal wishes. Too many therapists respond as if this is the intent and the patient is an adversary. Disguises for this reaction are criticizing the patient for being weak or threatening to call the police unnecessarily. The patient often calls because he or she wants, needs, and requests help. Too, the patient often wants to participate in getting help, and often has some good ideas of his or her own about what can be done. So ask, ''Is there something you would like me to do?'') All suicidal patients should be seen as soon as possible. There is no way to determine over the phone whether the patient is or is not suicidal. Schemes for doing so that rely on answers to the above or other questions are always unreliable.

3. As a symptom. The call is a symptom just as hand washing is a symptom. An example of symptomatic calling is the patient who called to say he was too obsessional to leave the house on time for his appointment and would be getting there late (after the therapist had left the office). Another example is the patient who called because he was too phobic to leave the house at all. (Some phobic patients can successfully be given enough initial treatment over the phone to allow them to eventually leave the house and begin therapy in the office.)

4. As acting out/resistance.

Example. A patient called to ask the therapist to push back his upcoming appointment five minutes. The therapist agreed but suspected the request was not as innocent as it sounded. In fact, buried in the innocent request was a transference opinion about the therapist. The patient wanted the appointment pushed back so that he could get to his next appointment on time. The next appointment was for a routine consultation with his mother's internist. The patient said about his mother's internist, ''I have to be there on time because he is an important doctor, whose schedule deserves respect.''

In other forms of acting out, the patient may call because he or she cannot face the therapist with material that shames him or her, or because he or she wishes to tell the therapist something without giving the therapist opportunity or time to respond. Some call so that they may speak to the therapist without having to pay him or her. (Therapists, unlike many attorneys, rarely charge for phone calls, and sometimes should.) The therapist must insist that such material not be considered adequately handled until brought back into a session. At the next session the therapist will mention the phone call, ask the reason for it, and ask the patient to discuss or rediscuss its content. The patient may be asked to associate to the phone call or its content just as he or she may be asked to associate to a dream.

5. Good news. Of course, the patient who calls the therapist to give him or her good news is, while perhaps overly naive and innocent, more healthy and mature than otherwise.

Meeting the Patient in Public Places

The therapist who has something to hide, or the therapist who is paranoid but has nothing to hide, will be especially fearful of meeting his or her patient in public places. Such a therapist might feel more comfortable living in a big city than in a small town; or he or she may choose to live in a small town, behaving "square" at home and doing his or her acting up out of town, where probably the only witnesses will be strangers.

Just as patients may provoke inadvertent meetings with therapists, therapists overly attached to/enamored of/dependent on their patients may provoke inadvertent meetings with their patients, for example, by deliberately using the same supermarket. The therapist who needs to meet with patients outside of office hours should explore the reasons (e.g., loneliness, inappropriate sexual attraction), seek changes in his or her own life, and perhaps seek therapy if unable to conquer the problem on his or her own.

In some professional circumstances (analyst/analysand relationships, for example), therapist-patient contact is an unavoidable fact of life. The therapist then will relax and behave normally, assured that the patient's observations of his or her behavior will, with a bit of care, invariably say more about the patient than they do about the therapist.

Of course, the therapist who meets his or her patient in extraordinary places will find his or her behavior as important an issue as that of the patient. In such cases the therapist may admit his or her preferences/pathology, assure the patient that in his or her opinion the preference/pathology does not interfere with the therapeutic work, and politely decline to discuss matters further.

Example: A therapist spotted in a gay bar was able to assure one patient that his presence there had little to do with treatment of the patient's mania with lithium, but unable to assure another patient that his presence there had little to do with his ability to treat the patient's professed suffering about his sexual orientation difficulty.

The worst thing you can do when inadvertently meeting a patient in a "revealing" place is to act as if you have not seen the patient. Always say hello, or the patient will wonder, Am I not good enough to be talked to outside of treatment? And do not try to hide, ostrich fashion, by staring off into space, or try to flee by turning a corner. Admit it; you have been spotted, even though the polite or frightened patient tries to look away. In the next session you might divert attention from yourself by asking for the patient's fantasies and distortions. But never try to lie, and do not blame the patient for coming to all-too-obvious conclusions. Do not hint that the patient is mean spirited or dereistic. In a particularly destructive example of therapist lack of truthfulness, a therapist "caught" by one of his patients with a younger homosexual companion made matters worse when he asked the patient, "Do you know for certain that that wasn't my son?" then wondered if the patient's suspicion was his way of expressing the patient's own homosexual fantasies.

The defensive therapist should remember, before becoming excessively defensive, that we are all human after all, and perfect therapy does not require a perfect therapist. Of this you may inform your hypercritical (often because of being frightened) patient.

Indeed, many therapists have emotional problems, and most have emotional problems that are contained and do not cause the patient difficulty. What causes difficulty is the tendency to display the emotional problems you have. This is a separate tendency, symptomatic of such character pathology as exhibitionism, masochism, and hypomania. If you cannot suppress your pathology, if you have to display your quirks, if you have to purposely disrupt treatment out of a self-punitive need to fail as a therapist, or if you are too "high" to see that your pathology shows and/or prevent it from showing, then you need to get help. Most patients are intolerant, not of the therapist who has a problem, but of the therapist whose problem is that he or she does not mind acting crazy. Less often they believe, He can't help himself, so how can he help me? More often they believe, He doesn't even recognize he has a problem and doesn't try to suppress it. Why should I?

Chapter 11

Transference and Countertransference

Therapy may stall or deteriorate when the patient and therapist lose sight of the presenting problem because either or both have become interlocked in a relationship more personal than professional, more infantile than mature, more negative than positive.

In the first part of this chapter, the reader will find a discussion of *countertransference* and *transference* and suggested ways to recognize and handle countertransference and transference problems, especially transference resistances. All terms are to be defined.

Because different disorders present unique patterns of transference, transference illness, and transference resistance, each requiring special handling, in the second part of this chapter representative examples of diagnosis-dependent negative and positive trends considered likely to be the subject matter of negative and positive transference, transference illness, and transference resistance are identified. Specific methods are suggested to handle resistances, avoid the development of or to dissipate these trends—the goal being to discourage all negative transference and transference illness, and positive transference and transference illness when used as a resistance.

DEFINING TERMS

The terms *countertransference* and *transference* are umbrella terms that gloss over a number of different therapist-patient interactions, here described individually. Three are described from the viewpoint of the therapist and three from the viewpoint of the patient, as follows.

The Problem From Where the Therapist Sits

True countertransference

1. The countertransference response. Countertransference is a semidelusional assessment of and reaction to an experience with a patient based on information obtained from another, related, past, or present experience from the therapist's life. We view the patient as we viewed our parents when we were children. Or we view the patient like another individual from our present life, either one who represents a threat or one who represents a consolation.

Since we are all human, we all have countertransference responses to all of our patients. They make us angry or stimulate us sexually. Only when we have a countertransference neurosis (countertransference illness), that is, when we relive a complex (an interlocked set) of our emotional problems with our patients, are we reacting inappropriately, nonproductively, and/or counterproductively.

Some of us have special countertransference problems with certain of our patients. Some of us cannot work with depressed patients (we find them too depressing), while others do not mind depressed patients but feel challenged or threatened by suspicious, paranoid patients. One therapist found a depressed patient "too passive for me to admire him" but surprisingly liked the spunk of a paranoid patient who, eager to reassure himself that the therapist was competent (i.e., not defective), and professional (i.e., not getting personal), tortured the therapist endlessly for minute details of his training and experience.

2. Acting-out the countertransference response. This might take such forms as the grandiosity of self-gratifying but unhelpful treatment (too flashy, too academic), depressive overpassivity and permissiveness, sadism (with impatience, use of inappropriate psychoactive drugs, punitive expulsion), masochism (with unrealistic attempts at cure), and/or obsessive overcontrol and domination.

3. Questions the therapist might ask about handling the countertransference response.

a. Is it all right to feel or get angry with our patient? Yes, but not too much and not too often. And you have to apologize. The patient may be told, "Though I feel angry because you got to me, either because you are good at this or I was too sensitive, or both, I don't plan on doing more than expressing my anger in passing, and I won't act on it in a way that will interfere with my therapy of you or hurt you. Also, accept my apologies."

b. Is it all right to have sexual feelings about the patient? Yes. But the patient can't be told of them because it is the rare (or nonexistent) patient who can handle this knowledge. The therapist whose sexual feelings are spotted should not lie and say, "I have none," but politely refuse to discuss the matter as being excessively personal and too easily subject to misunderstanding.

c. What do we do when we find our responses out of control? We might find ourselves, among other things, excessively troubled by, angry with, sexually attracted to, or overly eager to help a patient. The therapist should first try talking to colleagues and reading about others' similar experiences. He or she should then try self-analysis. A therapist mastered annoyance by self-analysis in the following case:

A therapist was annoyed by an obsessive-compulsive patient. The patient called to leave a message on the therapist's answering machine, called again to check that the machine picked up the message, called again to make sure the therapist didn't erase the message by mistake, and so forth. The therapist's annoyance diminished somewhat when he reached an understanding: "this patient reminds you of your father who, worried you might have a fever, would keep coming into your room in the middle of the night and take your temperature by kissing you on the forehead."

Finally, individual therapy may be indicated for what amounts to a work-related problem.

*False countertransference: the therapist's intellectual difficulties/
lack of talent look like countertransference problems*

Sometimes *countertransference response* really means "intellectual or technical problems." It is a simple fact of life that some therapists are brighter, more skilled, better trained, more interested, and/or more talented than others. The result is not countertransference irrationality but, what is different, relative or absolute technical failure. Rule: Care must be taken not to accuse the patient of being its cause.

*False countertransference: The patient's problems cause the
therapist to respond in a way that looks countertransferential but
is appropriate*

A therapist with a difficult patient should be distinguished from a therapist with countertransference and/or problems of intellect, skill, or training. Some patients are not presently candidates for treatment, while others are hard for everyone to treat. An example of the former is an unmotivated patient forced to be in treatment by his parents. An example of the latter is the so-called hand-me-down inpatient left over (so to speak) for the new residents each July. Another very difficult case: A therapist complained, "No matter what I do, my patient, natively intelligent and verbal, nevertheless keeps making noises instead of speaking. She says 'Mmmm' and 'Eh' and smacks her lips and tongue but doesn't say anything for minutes on end."

Some patients consciously or unconsciously intend to be especially provocative and know how to arouse us or get under our skin. Examples of typical provocations and possible to-be-expected responses are these:

1. The withdrawn schizoid patient, who makes us feel helpless because we

are unable to reach him or her, or defenseless because he or she is too remote to warm up to us enough to listen to what we have to say.

2. The quirky schizotypal patient, whose oddness provokes derision.

3. The blaming paranoid, who makes us feel attacked, defective, even depressed.

4. The *devaluing* borderline, who makes us feel worthless because he or she knows how to shatter our self-esteem. Also the *overvaluing* borderline who overinvolves us by trying to use us not as a therapist but as a companion.

5. The high and even assaultive manic, who makes us feel overwhelmed or in danger.

6. The perpetually despairing and ever-suffering depressive, who makes us feel helpless or makes us feel desperate when he or she sees our every offer of assistance as not enough.

7. The hypercritical passive-aggressive patient, who attacks us obliquely, makes us feel angry, then, because the provocation is so subtle, makes us feel guilty because we believe ourselves to be unjustifiably hypersensitive.

8. The clinging, dependent patient, who makes us feel pity but with anxiety about being drawn into a relationship we neither want nor feel we can handle.

9. The uncertain, ritualistic, weaving, stubborn obsessional, who makes us feel frustrated and exasperated.

10. The devaluing hysteric who makes us feel impotent by attacking us to retaliate when disappointed by our refusal to be seduced.

11. The manipulative psychopathic/antisocial patient, who makes us feel used by tricking us. (Being used is acceptable when neither hostile nor manipulative. An example is late-night telephone calls by an anxious, decompensating patient when these are not an expression of the patient's sadistic wish to annoy the therapist or an attempt to get thrown out of treatment, and when not simply a convenience because the patient works at night.)

The Problem From Where the Patient Sits

True transference

Transference is the patient's semidelusional assessment of and reaction to an experience with the therapist based on information obtained from another, related, past, or present experience. For example, when we speak of a parental transference to a therapist, we often mean that the patient falsely concludes that the therapist is *now* like his or her mother was *then*. Or the patient might see the therapist, not as a figure from his or her past, but as another figure from his or her present. He or she might believe, You are like my boss, or, You are like my jailer.

Transference illness is a semidelusional assessment of the totality of the therapeutic experience based on information obtained from the totality of another related, past, or present experience, when this other experience contributes to the patient's present illness. If the patient's present illness appears in symptomatic form as delusions of persecution derived from parental abuse, he or she perceives us as an adversary; or if the patient's present illness appears in symptomatic form as depression, he or she believes we are condemning and criticizing—just like his or her own mother and/or father. (The term *transference illness* is better than the term *transference neurosis,* since the present illness may be a personality disorder or a psychosis, not a neurosis.)

Much transference and transference illness has both negative and positive components, that is, is a mixture of love and hate. Sometimes one trend *prevails,* as with ingratiating psychopaths or ingratiating dependent patients. Sometimes negative and positive trends are *mixed* (ambivalence). Sometimes one *covers* the other, as when manifest hostility covers love (often the patient is reliving the hostile arm of a mixed relationship with a basically loved parent), or manifest love covers hostility, as when the patient uses positive feelings to seduce a therapist with whom he or she is angry. Sometimes negative and positive *alternate,* as with borderline patients who swing between positive and negative poles depending on whether you are being devalued or overvalued, or with cyclothymic patients who swing between negative and positive poles depending on their prevailing mood.

Sometimes the transference illness is so special, so characteristic, that it is diagnostic. Borderline patients, according to Arnold Modell (1963), have such a characteristic transference. The borderline patient relates to the therapist, accepting or rejecting the therapist as if he or she were a real person in the patient's life. The therapist becomes, for example, a potential real enemy or a potential real mate. In a case supervised and presented by Dr. Elizabeth Zetzel, the patient announced after a long, seemingly routine analysis, "We've been talking for five years now. Isn't it about time you divorced your wife so that you can marry me?"

False transference: the patient's real limitations appear to be transference problems

Here therapeutic problems have a nontransferential basis. The patient fails to improve because he or she has an untreatable illness or has allowed a treatable illness to progress too far and his or her condition to deteriorate. The patient might have suffered permanent damage from prior treatment. He or she might have an uncooperative family, an impossible spouse, or insufficient resources.

False transference: the therapist's problems cause the patient to respond in a way that appears transferential but is appropriate

Real problems with the therapist cause real reactions in the patient, not to be confused with transference. Here we include the patient who correctly accuses his or her therapist of being seductive, hostile, or incompetent.

TWO RULES FOR THE USE OF TRANSFERENCE/
COUNTERTRANSFERENCE

Rule 1: Stay Away From Transference Material Whenever Possible

The advice given to the beginner is the opposite of the advice that the therapist should be a blank screen upon which the patient will project his or her deepest wishes and fears. Instead, the beginning therapist is clearly warned of the dangers inherent in encouraging transference. Do not do it even for the seemingly innocent purpose of studying and analyzing its content.

The reason for the advice is as follows:

The beginning and moderately advanced therapist will work most comfortably and effectively with nontransference material, that is, with significant conflicts, anxieties, trends, complexes, and so on, appearing and expressed outside of the relationship with the therapist.

This notwithstanding, working with transference material has at least two significant advantages: (1) like any significant material, it is valuable for teaching the therapist about his or her patient; (2) like any significant material, it may be the content of clarifications, interpretations, and so on.

Working with transference material, however useful, has at least three significant disadvantages: (1) transference is often, because it is highly charged, too threatening to discuss with the patient. For example, much transference material is embarrassing and guilt-evoking; (2) transference response is fantasy. Fantasy avoids reality, for example, the therapist's real, not imagined, purpose; (3) transference provokes countertransference, often diversionary, sometimes disruptive.

Rule 2: Positive Is Sometimes No Better Than Negative

We can all understand how a negative trend becomes a resistance that interferes with therapy, and we can all understand how we should dissipate as much negative transference and transference illness as possible. But not all of us recognize that positive transference can be as much of a snare as negative. While it is all right to let positive transference and transference illness "ride" when it is not used as a resistance, *positive transference that is a resistance must be dispatched as quickly and efficiently as negative*.

We emphasize two circumstances in which the positive transference has become a resistance that interferes with therapy, that is, in which the positive relationship should be treated like a symptom—identified as problematic and removed by suitable intervention.

1. There is ambivalence, and the positive trend both covers and expresses the negative. For example, ingratiating behavior may both cover and express hostility; or clinging behavior, the sadistic demands of excessive dependence.

Example. A patient regularly congratulated her therapist for being like a mother to her. By this she meant that "my mother was there whenever I needed her." The therapist, realizing that this patient would start calling in the middle of the night when anxious and alone, then would interrupt treatment when the therapist inevitably complained, told her from the start, "I am not your all-giving mother. I am only a transitional figure meant to help you find dependable, satisfying relationships elsewhere."

2. The positive relationship repeats an aspect of the patient's disorder. Examples include schizophrenic regressive symbiosis, depressive dependence, and Oedipal, hysterical seductiveness.

This said, some positive transference, such as symbiosis with the therapist, may be fostered as a technique of support. The therapist does this when he or she has concluded that (a) this is the best the patient can do and (b) the alternative is severe regression and/or decompensation.

Warnings: (1) Seductiveness can never be fostered as a technique of support, or for any other reason. (2) Any positive counterresponse should be at most verbal/symbolic. The seductive patient, no matter how appealing, or the sick, regressed patient, no matter how needy, must be met with a degree of professional aloofness. One can say, "I promise to be available for your psychological needs for as long as you need me." One can say, "Here is some medicine as a token of my concern for you." But it is abuse to respond to the patient in kind. No therapist should ever have an affair with a patient, and no therapist should ever take the patient home to nourish him or her.

A Word about the Psychotic Transference

Psychotic patients might become delusional, not semidelusional, about the therapist. The "might be" and "as if" drops out: The patient no longer thinks, You might be my enemy and are acting as if you are my adversary, but rather, You are my enemy and my adversary. There is the possibility that the patient will incorporate the therapist into the patient's delusional system. The therapist might be incorporated into suspicious delusions, grandiose delusions (i.e., that the therapist is in love with the patient), and depressive delusions (i.e., that the therapist despises the patient). Negative signs warning of psychotic transference include excessive anger at the therapist or accusations about the therapist's malfeasance or incompetence. The patient might threaten to quit or threaten to assault the therapist. Positive signs warning of psychotic transference include a wish for excessive contact and the presence of excessive dependency. The patient might fall in love with the therapist then project and accuse the therapist of rape. Fortunately, many patients encapsulate both their negative and positive delusions and work around them. They might believe, This man is definitely my enemy, but with his credentials he can still do me a great deal of good.

Treatment of psychotic transference consists of confrontative reality reminders (such as, "No that's not so at all; you are a victim of your emotions that are so intense that understandably they create false belief''), reality testing (''You and I don't agree; let's identify our differences and explore the reasons for them''), obtaining consultation (not only because it is indicated but also because it has the effect of diluting the transference), medication (for the outpatient who is still cooperative), hospitalization, even interruption of therapy. The latter might have to be swift and abrupt, to spare the patient and the therapist the further pain of prolonging an unworkable, rapidly deteriorating, often dangerous relationship.

Other people in the patient's life may have to be informed that the patient is doing poorly, decompensating, posing a danger to him- or herself or to others. (In the long run this is a therapeutic, not punitive, response.)

IN SUMMARY

1. The beginning therapist is warned of the dangers inherent in artificially encouraging transference material, for example, so that it may be analyzed.

2. The beginning therapist is warned of the problems associated with positive as well as negative transference. We all know how negative transference can interfere with treatment. But many of us fail to realize how positive transference can be just as disruptive.

3. The beginning therapist is advised to dissipate as much negative transference or transference illness as possible and to let positive transference or transference illness ''ride,'' but only when it is not used as a resistance.

EXAMPLES OF HANDLING TRANSFERENCE RESISTANCE

We cite some examples from the schizophrenic and paranoid spectrum.

Schizophrenic Spectrum—Transference Manifestations/ Resultant Resistances

We group these according to descriptive, developmental and dynamic factors:

Descriptive

Here we focus on Eugen Bleuler's description of schizophrenia:

The Four As of Eugen Bleuler (1950). Bleuler's four As (example: ambivalence), plus Bleuler's secondary (restitutive) symptoms (example: delusions) help describe schizophrenic transference/transference illness and the resulting resistances to treatment, as follows:

1. Loosening of associative linkages. Thinking is disorganized. This can cause the patient to wander from the point (be tangential); never finish a thought (be circumstantial); or be fragmented in his or her thinking, becoming vague, confusing, and/or incomprehensible; and, unable to think clearly enough to concentrate, inattentive and/or uncomprehending.

2. Autism. A deficit in the ability to relate, often a manifestation of self-

preoccupation or self-centeredness. This makes the patient distant and remote, attuned to inner, not outer, stimuli/events.

3. Ambivalence. Opposite tendencies lie side by side. This makes the patient impulsive and unpredictable. As an example, a patient came to family therapy with his parents. As soon as the interview began, he got up and left the room. He was gone exactly 45 minutes, until the session was over. As the parents were getting up to leave, he returned, sat down, and said he was ready to start.

4. Disorder of affect. Amplitude of affect may be diminished, so that affect is blunted or flat. This makes the patient emotionally unresponsive. Sometimes mood is poorly regulated and thus labile. The mood changes rapidly and may be inappropriate to the expressed idea. Anhedonia may be present, with resultant disinterest not only in life but also in treatment.

Bleuler's secondary symptoms Bleuler saw such symptoms as delusions and hallucinations as secondary, really restitutive. (A delusion might restore, in fantasy, the patient's tendency to be isolated, in reality.) Delusions and hallucinations can make the patient suspicious, hostile, dangerous, or grandiose in his or her expectations of treatment.

Developmental

Here we focus on the patient's earlier relationship with the parents. The patient might avoid treatment because of terror about what the therapist might do, based on his or her early experiences with the mother and/or father, some of which are as follows:

Parental double-binding. The parents present the patient with contrary alternatives, both unacceptable, forcing a choice between Scylla and Charybdis. (A simple, terrifying example of a double bind is the therapist's duty to report homicidal threat without protection from breach of confidence.) Schizophrenia can become the only way out.

Parental overwhelming and emotional cannibalism, resulting in loss of identity (loss of the sense of an independent self) and loss of ego boundaries (loss of the sense of where the self begins and ends).

Parental infantilization with prolonged immaturity.

Dynamic

Here we mention ther dynamics of anger. Intense anger is paradoxically often associated with fear of dependency. The patient is maybe hostile to the therapist in order to avoid later rejection.

Intense anger may be handled by the overuse of the defense of projection, being projected along with forbidden homosexual wishes. An example is the patient who believed computer rays from a woman's college, rays unleashed by the female therapist, were burning into her sexual organs.

Schizophrenic Spectrum—Resultant Resistances

These are discussed with transference manifestations.

Schizophrenic Spectrum—Therapeutic Approach

Do not expect your patient to act like a neurotic patient. Bypass, rather than analyze resistance, when possible. For example, regular sessions may be out of the question. You might tell the patient, not, "Let's find out why you can't come regularly," but, "I'll see you when you are up to it. Give me a call and a little notice." Consider saying, not, "You are an adult; you can come without your father," but, "Ask your father to bring you whenever you feel depressed or anxious."

The patient needs many of his or her resistances/defenses/symptoms and is too ill to give them up, so set your sights relatively low, keep your goals modest, and follow the advice of Dr. Jerome Weinberger (personal communication), who saw therapy of the schizophrenic patient as a process of, "telling the patient what he or she needs to know in order to survive." Be willing to settle for adjustment with deficit, exemplified by the following outcome:

The "cure" for a hospitalized schizophrenic patient consisted of his returning to the community in the following state of compromised mental health: he was withdrawn from contacts with others, gave up his work as a waiter, and hardly went out of the apartment. He lived in an apartment furnished with tattered furniture, the light blocked out by screens covering the windows. His only relationships were with four Siamese cats and a roommate, a young woman who helped pay the rent but who disappeared for days or weeks. When she was home, they slept in shifts, he during the day, she at night, on a single bed. He stayed awake at night making collages of old movies on videotape. His self-esteem rested on the delusional belief that one day his tapes would make him rich and famous.

When necessary, seek help from such ancillary treatments as pharmacotherapy and hospitalization.

Paranoid Spectrum—Transference Manifestations

Included here are paranoid schizophrenia, true paranoia, and paranoid personality disorder. Also included are paranoid attitudes consistent with normal ones.

Transference manifestations of paranoia include anger, suspiciousness, and feelings of persecution. We see also nonaffective (persecutory) grandiosity, as, for example, in the idea, "I am the chief subject of your research on the mind's attention."

Transference fantasies can take one of two forms: (1) covert, because rationalized, with expression permitted, and (2) overt, with expression forbidden. An example of covert, rationalized, expressed, persecutory transference idea is found in the paranoid geriatric patient who stated (incorrectly), "I believe all my emotional complaints have a physical origin, and I want to leave treatment because you lack the credentials to handle my care." The following case is an example that illustrates overt unexpressed persecutory transference idea; it also illustrates a consequence of overlooking these unexpressed paranoid trends:

Example. A patient misdiagnosed as having an hysterical personality disorder was in twice a week insight-oriented psychotherapy. She was referred for control analysis to have more intensive uncovering treatment. The analyst, unlike the therapist, took notes during the session. It was the note-taking that brought the patient's paranoia to light. Seeing the analyst's note pad, the patient asked him to put it away, "Because note-taking gives my control over to the Martians."

Paranoid Spectrum—Resultant Resistances

The angry, suspicious, persecution-sensitive, persecution-expecting patient has not a therapist but a "defective adversary." He or she is not working on problems but attacking you for your flaws, inadequacies, and mistakes, and at the same time defending him or herself against your presumed assaultive ways.

Paranoid Spectrum—Therapeutic Approach

Three ways to reduce transference resistance are reality testing, setting limits, and honest discussion with abreaction.

Reality testing

Example. One therapist whose paranoid patient saw him as another father was blamed for intimidating the patient "like my father." The therapist was likely to become impotent because the patient saw each of his comments as "controlling my right to make my own decisions and live my life the way I want." It behooved this therapist not to encourage but to dissipate transference by telling his patient that he was *unlike* the patient's father, with different intentions, for example, and had no wish to be controlling.

Setting limits

In another case the therapist told an abusive paranoid patient not, "I believe we should look to the past to discover the origin of your need to devalue me," but, "I am not a punching bag, I can't take your hostility personally, and if you don't stop, then we will have to talk about alternatives to this treatment." This therapist did his patient a service by avoiding an unresolvable repetition of her hate-filled past relationship with her mother. By warning her that they were "participating in nothing," and should "take a rest from therapy" if the patient believed herself committed to this abusive, unhelpful interaction, the herapist prevented an intolerable and unresolvable relationship problem from developing in and interfering with therapy.

Honest discussion with abreaction

The wise, sensitive therapist knows that, to quote Dr. Robert Senescu (personal communication), "lilies that fester stink like weeds." He or she elicits and airs paranoid fantasies about him- or herself promptly, clearly, and unequivocally, then reassures the patient they are false. Most patients are not even aware of all the paranoid ideas or delusions that contaminate their transference. The therapist should not only assume some paranoia and expose each patient's special false ideas and delusions but should also make a list of typical ones, assume them to be present, and "torpedo" each one—presumed present until proved otherwise.

One therapist told each of his patients: "Most patients in treatment have false ideas that interfere with treatment. Should you detect such a false idea, please discuss it. As an example, I have found that many patients in long-term therapy believe that I continue treatment, not because they need it, but because I see them as an annuity and need the money. Of course, this *is* the way I make my living. But around these ounces of reality are pounds of elaboration that say, This is the *only* reason that you are in treatment. In fact I have a busy practice and won't keep you in treatment for longer than you need to be here. In this you can trust me. At any time I will give you, upon request, a progress report, including why I believe you still need treatment. I do this because I want you to see that I am behaving rationally, objectively, and in your best interests as well as in mine.

"Probably you will also think, I am angry with you, am about to report you to the authorities, am talking about you behind your back, am planning to give you drugs or hospitalize you against your will, etc. We all have such thoughts—the mind, like the heart, beats all the time, and sometimes beats irregularly, so to speak. Please discuss these ideas, no matter how silly they seem. I have heard everything before, and won't hold it against you."

The following case is illustrative of acting out of distrust that has been allowed to fester.

A homosexual patient in three-times-a-week psychotherapy for many years married, though still homosexual, for appearances when he attained an important administrative position. Soon afterward he suddenly and unexpectedly disappeared from treatment without a call or letter. The perplexed psychiatrist contacted him to ask what had happened, only to be told, "You must understand. I have a sensitive administrative position. I have to avoid you now because you know too much about me."

Do not, however, insist that the patient become too trusting. Too much basic trust leaves the patient unprotected in his or her potentially dangerous world, and with you.

REFERENCES

Bleuler, Eugen. *Dementia Praecox or the Group of Schizophrenias*. New York: International Universities Press, 1950.

Modell, Arnold H. Primitive object relationships and the predisposition to schizophrenia. *Int. J. Psychoanal.* 44: 282–291 (1963).

Senescu, Robert (personal communication).

Weinberger, Jerome (personal communication).

Chapter 12

Avoiding Common Therapeutic
Errors—Diagnostic

Because of therapist error the patient fails to improve, improves, then plateaus and stagnates, or, after stabilizing, gets worse. The errors may be intentional (sadistic) or unintentional; overt or covert; of omission or commission. An example of an error of omission is failure of empathy, an example of an error of commission is an inexact or incorrect interpretation. Some forms of therapy spawn certain errors, some others, with active therapies (i.e., behavioral) tending to spawn overt errors of commission and passive therapies (i.e., analysis) tending to spawn covert errors of omission.

Errors made by the therapist must be indentified for at least four reasons:

1. so that the therapist may admit error to him- or herself and change attitude, procedure, and so forth;

2. so that in selected cases the therapist may admit error to the patient;

3. so that the therapist can avoid repeating the same error with the same or next patient;

4. so that the therapist does not blame the error on the patient. An example is the therapist who fell asleep during a session, then said to the patient, "Why do you produce material so boring that it fails to keep me awake?"

In the four chapters in this section we list commonly made errors. The errors listed in the first three chapters of this section tend to occur in the treatment of all psychotherapy patients, regardless of diagnosis. These errors are broadly divided into diagnostic, technical, and emotional errors. Diagnostic and technical errors are those that primarily occur because of poor training, lack of knowledge, or lack of experience. Emotional errors (countertransference errors) are those that primarily occur because the therapist with a disordered personality trait, neurotic problem, or psychotic problem acts out his or her disorder with the patient. The errors listed in the fourth chapter of this section are diagnosis related, that is, they tend to occur in the treatment of patients with a specific diagnosis.

Since therapeutic errors are in some ways the obverse of therapeutic recommendations, there will be some overlap between the material in this section and material in the other chapters.

DIAGNOSTIC ERRORS

Examples

Four examples of incorrect diagnosis are the following:

1. A paranoid schizophrenic patient was believed to have a manic affective disorder when the therapist overlooked a paranoid delusion. Tragically, the patient was elated because, believing her dog, Onion, to be an enemy warlock, she had killed him, an act she considered a positive accomplishment.

2. A paranoid patient believed to have obsessional worries in fact was preoccupied with paranoid delusions. Sample delusional worry: He told his therapist a good joke he had heard from a waiter. Then he worried, The therapist is having a relationship with the waiter, will tell him the joke back, and the waiter will discover I am in psychotherapy.

3. A patient was believed to have the hypochondriacal obsessive fear that he was developing organic brain disease. In fact he had had a small stroke, first revealed after psychological testing.

4. A patient was believed to have an organic brain syndrome because he complained, "My memory is gone and I have Alzheimer's." But he was in fact organically intact, actually suffering from a fear of, or obsession with, Alzheimer's.

Some Reasons for Misdiagnosis

1. Having preconceived notions. Here the therapist proves his or her point by listening selectively, discouraging the production of facts contradictory to his or her preconceived notion, or interpreting facts the way he or she intends. Often, one part of a problem is emphasized while another obscured, one feature of an illness observed while another overlooked, usually a trivial aspect of an illness emphasized over one that is important. Examples: A delusion of being contaminated is misdiagnosed as a phobia of dirt or an obsessive fear of getting dirty. Or the obsessional need to "make even" is confused with the paranoid need to "get even."

Behaviorists more often err by focusing on an unimportant, trivial symptom of an important, significant illness (phobic symptoms in schizophrenics), cognitive therapists by emphasizing rational thought while overlooking irrational passion, and insight therapists by emphasizing the sleeping past over the awake, active, problematic, provocative present.

Rule: It is a simple truth that in the mental health professions you can prove almost any point you wish to make if you are motivated and clever.

2. Accepting the patient's self-diagnosis without doing a confirmatory diagnostic evaluation of your own. Take special care when the diagnosis given is the premise for a self-serving request for medication (e.g., benzodiazepines for the self-diagnosis of panic attacks, amphetamines for the self-diagnosis of narcolepsy).

3. Believing one side of the story. The therapist often hears one side of the story, rarely two. The patient's version of events is always at least partly false.

4. Failing to distinguish ego syntonic (wanted, liked) from ego dystonic (unwanted, unliked). The therapist confounds patients who embrace their feelings with patients who are at odds with them, so that the patient afraid of hostility is called hostile, or the patient at odds with an aspect of sexuality is called perverse.

5. Misinterpreting the significance of the patient's reality. As an example, a masochistic patient who needed to be encouraged to abandon a sadistic partner was instead told he was a paranoid patient imagining abuse. (This injudicious intervention caused the patient severe headaches and led to premature termination of treatment to avoid worsening depression.)

Rule: Always avoid assigning responsibility to the wrong person or circumstance. Avoid making the world responsible for something the patient did to him- or herself, or making the patient responsible for provoking his or her own fate when bad luck or unfortunate circumstances were responsible.

Example. In a case illustrating overlooking the importance of fantasy, a therapist became depressed when he overlooked the sadistic intent of persistent, unrealistic complaints about his office, complaints really designed (as the patients later admitted) to ''get you by the scruff of the neck and torture you with something you are powerless to alter.''

In a contrasting case illustrating overlooking the importance of reality, another therapist overlooked the reality of the complaints about his office even though the office was realistically too hot, there were no cups for water, no paper towels, no umbrella stand, and so on, and inappropriately accused the patient of being a malcontent.

Chapter 13

Avoiding Common Therapeutic
Errors—Bad Technique

This discussion of bad technique is divided into two sections: general technical errors and errors of clarification and interpretation.

BAD TECHNIQUE—GENERAL TECHNICAL ERRORS

Choosing an Inferior over a Superior Technique

Here the therapist chooses from two or more suitable approaches the one with the most disadvantages and the fewest advantages. For example, the therapist *analyzes* a phobia for which a *behavioral* approach might have been quicker and more effective. (It would also have been less complete, for example, unlikely to change associated symptoms, such as obsessions, or an underlying personality disorder, such as depression.)

Rushing the Patient

Therapy, like most things, takes time, because it has a natural course and so has to go at its own rate. The therapist can consciously decide to do short-term therapy, to limit the scope of therapy, or to bypass the need for therapy (e.g., with medication). But he or she cannot make long-term therapy into short-term therapy by rushing. When you become impatient, remember that there is often no reason to hurry to finish because the patient in therapy begins to improve before therapy is over.

The rushed therapist typically confuses the truly stagnant patient with one who seems stagnant but is in fact making progress—regrouping forces for the next assault on the symptoms or quietly consolidating and integrating previous gains (working through).

Being Too Real

While the days of the completely blank screen are perhaps over, some therapists are too real, too human. They let the patient in on their secrets, sometimes to seduce the patient into loving them because they are open and honest. They talk to their wives and lovers on the phone during a session (while maintaining the fantasy that the patient does not know who is on the other end of the phone), arrange during the session for workmen to come to their home, and so on.

An advantage of this approach is that the patient is disabused of antitherapeutic fantasies of the therapist as a suprahuman figure—as one who can read minds and so does not have to be told what the patient is thinking, is omniscient enough to understand everything without the patient having to explain it, has no feelings and can be abused at will, does not have financial commitments and so does not have to be paid, does not have a need for privacy and rest. A disadvantage of this approach is that therapists (and this is most therapists) who use suggestion in any of its forms will find that the patient, disabused of infantile magical expectations about the therapist, such as the fantasy that the therapist can work miracles, becomes less likely to blindly follow the therapist's helpful lead.

Being Too Apologetic

Some therapists equate humanity with self-abuse. When they make a mistake, instead of offering a simple apology, they overdo, depressively or masochistically acting the part of the sorrowful one. The patient thinks, not, What a nice, concerned person (as was the therapist's intention), but, Perhaps I have an incompetent therapist. In particular, narcissistic and paranoid patients need to believe their therapists infallible; and when invited to blame the therapist for making errors they will be tempted to find the therapist altogether no good because of the minor mistake. The patient will predictably throw out the baby with the bath water, totally condemning the therapist, usually in the service of the resistance.

Overusing Humor and Irony

Both, unless handled with consummate skill, give the impression the therapist is belittling the patient's problems and/or making fun of the patient.

Overtimidity

The therapist goes by the book; the therapist does not trust his or her own instincts. He or she speaks only with the imprimatur of authority—texts, supervisors, and so on. Not only does this therapist go by the book, but he or she takes the book too literally, often cruelly so. One therapist, after learning that short-term analysis consisted of analyzing Oedipus, no more, terminated treatment without handling any other material even though such problems as problems with control and dependency continued. Another therapist, too literal in his analytic orientation, treated his patient by "regression" (suggesting the patient be as infantile as she chose), then brought her "back to genitality" by sequential interpretations of perceived "oral, anal, and phallic fixations."

Forgetting the Time Frame

Many therapists tell a patient what to do but forget to tell the patient when to stop doing it. Outstanding is the giving of sleeping pills for temporary insomnia, then forgetting the patient is refilling the prescription.

Errors With the Fee

Overcharging

Overcharging wealthy patients can create resentment. While socially admirable, the therapist who overcharges the wealthy patient then tells him or her that the extra fee is going to make up for a reduced fee for those who cannot afford treatment creates transference stress, especially when you ask the wealthy *masochistic* patient to sacrifice for others.

Undercharging

We refer to undercharging the patient who can afford the fee but who falsely claims poverty, especially when the patient prefers to use his or her money for another activity, as, in one case, for building a country home. In an extreme example, a patient made a suicide attempt, taking 50 barbiturates. Her life was barely saved with renal dialysis. When the medical crisis was over, psychiatric hospitalization was recommended but refused, "Because I can't afford it." Confronted with a bank account of over $50,000 (quite a fortune in the days when this happened), the patient responded, incredibly, "That money is not to be used now: that is money I am saving for my old age."

Criticizing Others

Criticizing a patient's former therapist is forbidden. If you want to disagree say, "I don't see things in quite the same way," not, "He doesn't know what he is talking about.'' Never get drawn into a war between yourself and other practitioners. And remember that the M.D. who criticizes the psychologist (say, for incomplete training) can be as inappropriately sadistic as the non-M.D. who criticizes the psychiatrist (e.g., saying, ''All you can treat is psychotic patients with drugs; I'm better qualified to do psychotherapy'').

Refusal to Admit an Error You have Made

The therapist who makes an error compounds it when, after it is discovered, he or she hides or denies it. It is sometimes wise to admit one's inevitable failings and always better to do so than to put the patient in a double bind by (1) committing an error caught by the patient, (2) denying it though obvious, (3) invoking the privilege of divine authority to silence the patient's protests, and/ or (4) blaming the patient for facilitating or causing it.

Falling Asleep During the Session

No matter how tired you are, do not let yourself fall asleep. You can always control it, if you wish to do so. Especially, do not make the mistake of the psychopathic therapist who fell asleep then justified it by saying, ''It's an unparalleled opportunity to tell you of the dreams you stimulated in me.''

Timing Errors

Cutting the hour short

Do not think you are not being timed. If you have to cut the hour short, tell the patient you are so doing, why you are doing it, and offer to make lost time up the next session, or as soon afterward as possible.

Starting the hour too early or too late

Both are unacceptable. One therapist regularly scheduled his patients for on the hour then began a few minutes early, thinking, This way I will get the session over sooner. This predictably irritated some patients, for example, those who needed the time in the waiting room—to organize their thoughts, read notes, and so forth. (One such therapist had a mighty struggle with an obsessional patient who waited just until time was to begin before disappearing into the bathroom. This patient also went to the bathroom after the session was over— but only when he knew that his was the last session and the therapist was eager to close the office and leave.)

If the patient is late, and late for a real reason, for example, a snow storm, give the patient more time if you have it. If the patient is late because the patient delayed him- or herself (''I don't wear a watch and so never know what time it is . . . '') hold the patient to the scheduled end of the session. Be more flexible when the delay is more the product of illness (e.g., obsessive-compulsive hand washing) than of ill will ("I'm angry with you for implying that I'm crazy last session"). If uncertain which, try to give the patient the benefit of the doubt.

Not stopping on time

Regular sessions should stop on time, without the therapist apologizing. The cut-off patient may be permitted to wind up thoughts but not elaborate extensively, and certainly not permitted to begin another topic. A bit of "See you next time" small talk is permissible.

Keeping Secrets from the Patient

This is morally (not necessarily legally) acceptable only when the patient is not yet ready to hear information he or she cannot handle. If you can avoid it, do not collaborate with the patient's wife, boss, the government, or the patient's parents in a conspiracy of secrecy.

Problems with Empathy

Lack of empathy

Failing to see the patient wants or needs the disorder. The beginning therapist must learn to accept what is often a semifatal blow to his or her narcissism. The clinician who believes him- or herself to be an arbiter of what constitutes maladaptive symptomatic behavior, on the one hand, and what constitutes good function on the other, would do well to contemplate how in all but the most egregious circumstances, the definition of *maladaptive* is relative. It is obscured by a number of qualifying factors, including personal preference, comparative (often very personal) importance of such matters as money, and geographical and temporal circumstances (what is considered in one place at one time adaptive is considered in other places and at other times maladaptive). In particular, a personality disorder that catalyzes function can be more desirable than undesirable—for example, a psychopathic/antisocial disorder that is bad for relationships but "good for business," or a hypomanic personality disorder that enhances creativity.

Excessive empathy

Excessive empathy can take the form of listening with the third ear but not with the first two. The therapist reads between the lines but not the lines themselves. This leads to unwarranted inference or autistic conclusion. Everything has a hidden meaning, but nothing stands for itself.

Impoliteness

The therapist might answer the phone and talk too long or remove him- or herself by taking too many notes.

Overlooking the Importance of Hidden Messages

Preludes and postludes. Often more is said before a session begins or after a session ends than is said during the session. Some patients hide the significance of material by producing it before the session begins. Other patients afraid to be honest about hidden wishes and feelings during the session mention them after the session is over, when they sense it is too late for the therapist to be attentive to what they have said. Thus one hysterical patient murmured in passing after her session was over, "Perhaps I should see my internist to find out if this all from a physical problem." In this way the patient undid the entire session by relegating it to the archives of "not relevant."

Overlooking remarks made in passing. Side remarks, often made in humor, typically contain rich, concentrated, codified lode and should be noted, underscored by the therapist who may have to call the patient's attention to what has been said, and analyzed.

Mishandling Questions Asked by the Patient

Answering a question with a question

The patient asks, "Now what do you think?" and is answered with another question, "Now what do *you* think?" "Does it matter?" or, "Why do you ask?" Nobody else talks this way. It is off-putting and goes nowhere. Give the patient an answer or do not give one and say why, or ask for an elaboration of the patient's question. (An exception to this rule may exist in pure insight-oriented therapy.) You may want to adapt your answer to the specific disorder. For example, the therapist may say to a passive-aggressive patient, "I'll tell you what I think, but I hope you don't want to know what I think just so that you may think the opposite."

The therapist who parrots a question (or any other patient communication) perhaps does so with a new emphasis on one or more parts of the original. But what may be gained (e.g., clarification by reemphasis) is more than lost, because the therapist may seem peculiar and because the therapist probably can do better.

Attacking the Patient with a Question

In this forbidden passive-aggressive technique, the therapist believes his or her abuse of the patient is cleverly hidden by placing a question mark at the finish of an attack. One therapist asked his patient (who was about to marry a woman 25 years his junior), "What would a woman so young find interesting

in you?'' Such an attack can be denied by saying, ''It was only a question,''
but the sensible therapist should not expect his or her patient to buy the defense.
Also unlikely to be acceptable is the defense, ''I was merely trying to get at
your fantasies, so I was only doing it for your benefit.''

Failure to Maintain 105 Percent Confidentiality

Do not talk about, or write about, a patient without permission, even to another
therapist or to the patient's medical doctor. The exception is on an inpatient
service, where the patient should be told that anything he or she says is kept
confidential, not by one individual, but by the team.

Never tell the patient's story to your wife, husband, or lover. You may not
see them as an outsider, but the patient may. And never talk about patients in
the elevator or at dinner in a restaurant. You can usually be overheard, and even
when you believe you are disguising the case, the disguise, more often than you
think, is too thin to fool the hearer at the next table. (This is especially true in
small towns, where everyone knows everyone else.)

Often overlooked, but similar, is talking about one's other patients to the
present patient—even though well disguised. The therapist who uses his or her
other patients as examples frightens the patient at hand who correctly believes
that his or her problems will be the next ones used for examples.

Premature or Inappropriate Reassurance

Even though the patient asks to be told that everything will be all right, if
you reassure the patient prematurely, you may face resentment later. The patient
might believe, My therapist lulled me into a sense of security and failed to warn
me that I should make timely effort to correct a potentially dangerous situation.
Example: The warning, You are too paranoid, in some circumstances should
instead be, You are not paranoid enough.

Setting One's Goals Too Low

Here the therapist tells the patient to be satisfied with his or her lot when in
fact the therapist should be inspiring the patient onward and upward.

Setting One's Goals Too High

Not all people can or should work, can or should marry, or can or should
make their unconscious conscious.

Working over the Telephone

The therapist who works over the telephone is often participating in a resistance. Much useful but threatening material is presented on the phone because

the patient knows the therapist cannot or prefers not to talk about it. The patient who calls at night may do so, not to annoy the therapist after hours, but to confess safely, knowing the therapist will be too busy to reprimand. The patient feels, I haven't been derelict because after all I did talk about it. As noted previously, an exception may be made for the phobic patient who is too phobic to come to the therapist's office and for the obsessive-compulsive patient who is trapped at home having to do rituals. Here phone sessions in the beginning may reduce anxiety enough to permit the patient to travel to the office for further treatment.

Doing Therapy When You Do Not Feel Well

Some therapists do therapy when temporarily incapacitated, then fail to mention they are sick or tired. They should explain this to the patient and ask the patient for his or her indulgence. Otherwise the patient will either blame him- or herself or believe the therapist is losing his or her skills. If the session will be compromised, the therapist may proceed and not charge the patient, proceed and charge the patient less (depending on the extent of the incapacity), or cancel the session, even shortly after it starts.

Of course, humanitarian, medicolegal, and commonsense considerations forbid that the therapist run a session after taking alcohol or drugs.

Bad Timing

Try to make your comments relevant to the patient's train of thought. Do not interrupt the session to insert something that suddenly comes to mind. However, the time is never right for some things. And time has to be made for those matters for which there is no right time. An announcement of a vacation, discussion of an unpaid bill, and so on, has to be inserted when you can—when there is a pause or, with patients who do not pause, by starting to talk at the beginning of the patient's next sentence.

Failure to Explain

The typical therapist, familiar with the process of therapy, fails to appreciate how the typical patient misunderstands and thus distorts both the therapeutic process and the specific statements the therapist makes. The typical therapist does not tell the patient how to work in therapy, assumes he or she knows, then incorrectly identifies deviations caused by ignorance as resistances. This therapist makes statements without elaborating enough, without sufficiently explaining to the patient how he or she has arrived at certain conclusions, why he or she is making a particular comment, and what he or she both does and does not mean by the comment. For example, a therapist who said, "You have a subtle way of putting the knife in to your wife," was trying to clarify a passive-aggressive

technique used by his patient. (The therapist intended to emphasize "subtle.")
But the patient heard, "You are the one putting the knife into her," so concluded
he was guilty and thought the therapist was taking the wife's side. This could
have been avoided if the therapist had qualified his statement with, "Of course,
I'm not blaming or criticizing you or affixing responsibility; I call your attention
to this aspect of the problem to point out a difficulty you have with expressing
your anger directly." This way the patient's reactive anger and disappointment
could have been muted or avoided. Rule: Every important clarification and
interpretation should, at least the first time, be qualified/explained in much the
same way.

BAD TECHNIQUE—ERRORS OF CLARIFICATION AND INTERPRETATION

Premature Clarification and Interpretation

Flooding the patient

Some therapists are so excited about what they learn that they cannot wait to
convey what they know to their patient. This approach of interest and zeal is
not commendable when it floods the patient, for example, by removing a needed
defense or removing one symptom, such as a depressive symptom, that defends
against another, more serious symptom, such as a paranoid delusion.

Never forget that what is old material with no impact for the therapist who
has heard it all before is new material with fresh impact for the patient who is
hearing it for the first time. Never forget that material that is bland for the
therapist because he or she is not personally involved is emotionally loaded for
the patient because he or she *is* personally involved.

Interpretive Errors

The wrong interpretation

Example. A therapist told his depressed patient, "You internalize rage because
of guilt about your anger." In fact the rage was internalized out of love: out of
a wish to spare the partner from anger correctly perceived by the patient as
excessive.

Example. A patient would not allow his mother to have his address or phone
number because he believed she would use them to take over his life. The
therapist suggested that this was a manifestation of the patient's fear of being
orally controlled. Months later the patient told the therapist, "You were wrong;
see, she is calling my brother and my sister in the middle of the night. That's
why I didn't want her to have my number."

Partially correct/incorrect interpretations

Interpretations are often but partially correct. They might overlook the contribution of reality to fantasy or emphasize sexual motivation over hostile, or the other way around.

Chapter 14

Avoiding Common Therapeutic Errors—Countertransference Acting-Out

INTRODUCTION

In countertransference acting-out the therapist relives aspects of his or her emotional problems or disorder with the patient. Sometimes the acting out originates mainly with the therapist; sometimes the therapist is provoked into it, for example, by an angry, seductive, or demanding patient. The countertransference acting-out is more likely to occur when the patient has chosen either a *therapist* who is just like the mother or father or a *mode of treatment* that is like something about the mother or father. For example, a patient selected Freudian analysis in an attempt to repeat a relationship with a silent father. Problems can also occur when patients select a therapist or a mode of treatment the opposite of a crucial element in their relationship with a parent. For example, a patient selected behavior therapy because the therapist's activity (as distinct from passivity) showed him that she cared.

Countertransference acting-out problems broadly fall into two categories: positive and negative. Examples of positive countertransference problems are coddling and infantilizing the patient. These behaviors may appear in such guises as excessive symbolic feeding, overtreating, failure to discipline out of a misguided sense of caring, or overfamiliarity. The overfamiliar therapist might enter into business with the patient, for example, as a financial partner, or ask the patient to do chores, for example, if the patient is a handyman, having him or her work around the house, perhaps instead of payment. Examples of negative countertransference are mistreating, abandoning, or being sadistic to the patient. This can be done by omission, for example, failure to speak out against a patient's impulsive behavior, or by commission, for example, giving the patient the wrong advice in an unconscious attempt to hurt him or her. Usually countertransference hatred is subtle and difficult to detect. A therapist competed with his patients, wistfully complaining to them, "All my patients are doing better than I am"— not really the point. But sometimes it is surprisingly overt. One therapist sadistically ordered a patient capable of being independent about, failing to leave the decision to have psychoanalysis up to the patient and cajoling, overselling, and insisting that he "get treatment because otherwise you are guaranteed to end up emotionally paralyzed."

PERSONAL PROBLEMS THAT CAN APPEAR IN TREATMENT

Paranoid Traits

Here the therapist might become overly suspicious of the patient's intent, for example, seeing all cancellations as personal slights. The therapist might assume malignant intent, for example, believing the patient who is late in paying is out to gyp him or her of his or her fee, or believing the merely dissatisfied patient is planning to sue.

Schizotypal Traits

This can present itself as acting or being odd. An example is espousing odd, peripheral medical theories such as the idea that mercury fillings in one's teeth create emotional disorder by creating mercury blood poisoning. (Sometimes it is hard to tell if a theory is peripheral—for example, the idea that riding backward on the train makes you sick.)

Grandiose or Depressive Traits

Grandiosity can take a number of forms, sometimes subtle (the depressed therapist may do the opposite—where applicable):

1. Overconfidence. In one therapist, overconfidence appeared as failure to keep records. The therapist believed, I can remember everything my patients say.

2. Hostility to others who are deemed inferior because they are believed stupid. This may take the form of overarguing with the patient or with colleagues on the therapeutic team.

3. Overzealousness and therapeutic heroism owing to grandiose goals or expectations.

4. Overfondness for a particular theory or therapy (not odd or peripheral as with the schizotypal therapist). One therapist believed that *all* manifestations of *all* affective disorder, including reactive depression, were entirely chemical, with no emotional component.

5. Pomposity. The therapist acts the role of Providing Mother, saint, guru, or God, manifest in such behaviors as highfalutin, ringing, holy speech that mystifies or offends as much as it impresses.

6. Self-deification. The therapist may try to convey to the patient, or fail to disabuse the patient of, the fact that he or she is in the presence of a suprahuman figure with supernatural powers. (Such a therapist may be able to use techniques such as suggestion, the giving of advice, manipulation, hypnosis, better than his or her less grandiose fellow, but this therapist creates other problems, typically a fall in self-esteem in depressed patients who compare themselves unfavorably to their therapist, believed to be grander, more powerful, less human, and more divine. In one case a therapist, during the therapy hour, gave a patient a tour of his (admittedly beautiful) 27–room mansion. (That night the patient thought, "He's an important person. I'm not.")

7. Autocracy. Many patients would become the therapist's ally in a quest for health if only the therapist would permit. Many therapists instead do *to* the patient. They invariably fail to harness one of the best sources available for getting information and producing cure—the patient's own tendency toward health, a tendency that often leads the patient, if given a chance, to side and cooperate with the therapist. Sessions should ideally contain a number of therapist statements meant to elicit peer cooperation, as, "Now what would you say to that, if you were I?" or, "Let's look at that together and explore it as adults."

8. Control. Some therapists run roughshod over the patient's self-generated positions or standards, imposing their own. They respect neither the patient's own will nor his or her uniqueness or originality.

Example. One patient demanded his money back when the flowers he ordered for Mother's Day were delivered a day late. He felt, "I paid for Mother's Day flowers, and my Mother should have gotten them on Mother's Day, not the day after." The therapist disagreed. "You shouldn't make such a big deal over such a small matter. Simply overlook the incident, then don't return to the store again."

Example. A psychiatrist, with appalling immodesty, told his doctor patient, "Don't go into surgery; go into dermatology: it's more suited to your personality."

9. Experimental cuteness. The therapist tries clever techniques, often simplistic, even derived from concrete thinking. An example is treatment of a hallucinating patient by placing a personal stereo on the patient's head with a tape prepared to counter disturbing voices. Mostly wish-fulfilling, not only did it not work, but it presented the therapist as silly, rendering him less effective in other aspects of the patient's case.

10. Mysteriousness. Often grandiose is the mysterious, pure therapeutic "experience." The therapist isolates him- or herself with the patient; refuses to accept phone calls, believed to be contaminating; complains of minor interferences (such as footsteps upstairs); and will not allow even a small interruption of the session, say for a drink of water or an emergency trip to the bathroom.

11. Hypomanic behavior. One hypomanic analyst for no apparent reason lifted the patient's head from the couch in midsession to change the mat under the patient's head.

Sadomasochistic Traits

All therapies, can, when misused, be hurtful. Examples include not only organic modes such as ECT (when sadistic) or drugging (when punitive) but also life-sapping overanalysis, behavior therapy when there is an unconscious intention to brainwash, or cognitive therapy misused because the therapist is unconsciously argumentative.

Obsessive-Compulsive Traits

1. Excessive fussiness. This appears as an internally meaningful but relatively unproductive activity, a luxury even when affordable.

For example, we cite the perhaps excessive analysis of the following symptom: When giving a party, the patient believed herself compelled to remove a portion of the food she ordered, freeze it, and save it for herself to use at a later date. Exploration revealed that the patient especially withheld portions of smoked salmon to eat later. The therapist reminded the patient that the smoked salmon was purchased for her by her sister, who got a food discount at the school where she taught. The therapist made the interpretation that withholding the smoked salmon was a manifestation of her oral dependent relationship with her sister.

2. Excessive neutrality. Here the obsessional therapist remains a neutral blank screen, not for considered technical reasons, but because of being a perfectionist afraid to make an error. The therapist becomes too passive, fails to extend needed support, or makes deep psychological interpretations just to avoid giving helpful advice (even when obvious and needed).

Example. A patient with a subway phobia complained that he panicked when in a crowded train that stopped between stations. His therapist analyzed the phobia as due to a fear of being trapped in a primal scene. Out of a rigid moral belief that it was "unchristian" to bypass a neurosis and that giving advice contaminated the transference and prevented resolution of the fundamental problem, assuring symptom return or substitution, the therapist never supported the patient's own suggestion that he move so that he could walk to work.

Hysterical Traits

A sexual attraction to and seduction of a patient may occur. In a case of hysterical disorder the therapist's desire can hark back to unresolved Oedipus, the forbidden patient substituting for the forbidden parent. Other forms of seduction have to be distinguished, particularly the following six:

1. Schizophrenic. The therapist may have a delusion that leads him or her to believe the patient is a love object.

2. Borderline. The borderline therapist falls in love with his or her patient, not because the patient is forbidden, like Mother or Father, but because he or she overvalues the patient.

3. Depressive. Depressed people often like others who are "one down." "One down" people need them and do not threaten their already low self-esteem by competing. The depressed therapist may feel love for the person identified as one down because of the person being a patient.

4. Hypomanic. The therapist who is high would not care if the love object is a patient.

5. Psychopathic. The therapist who is amoral would not care if the love object is a patient.

6. Impulsive. The therapist cares but has poor control.

Psychopathic Traits

The psychopathic therapist uses the patient for his or her own needs—for the money, as an object for research, or, as above, for sex.

Impulsive Traits

Manifestations of poor impulse control include these:

1. Too many hostile or sexual Freudian slips. One angry competitive therapist intending to express thanks to his patient said, revealingly, "I will be thankful to you until the day *you* die" (italics supplied).

2. Loss of temper. The therapist who snaps at the patient should always extend an apology, even though the loss of temper was provoked. The apology may (or may not) be followed by a discussion of the provocation. But even temporary loss of temper, though perhaps understandable, can doom treatment. One patient said to his analyst, "We don't seem to be getting along very well," and the analyst, momentarily fed up with the patient, shot back, "I agree. You should quit." Such a remark, made in haste, can only be repented at leisure, probably after the patient has been provoked to terminate. Apologies may not be accepted, and this may not be because the patient "needed something to complain about or quit over anyway."

3. Tastelessness. The impulsive therapist may make tasteless jokes, be ironic—usually inappropriate and usually sadistic—and/or make fun of the patient. The therapist may speak crudely, for example, using four letter words of his or her own (i.e., not to reflect back the patient's own four-letter words).

Chapter 15

Avoiding Common Therapeutic
Errors—Specific Syndrome Errors

SCHIZOPHRENIA

1. Infantilizing. The therapist should resist pressure to infantilize the patient.

Example. A mother, herself emotionally dependent on a schizophrenic child, saw her child's growing up as a threat, so tried to convince the child's therapist that the child could not survive on his own. The unsophisticated therapist sided with the infantilizing mother without realizing that the child was sick in the first place because of the mother's attitude.

Example. Each year this patient's mother, on New Year's Day, would say to her daughter, "D., this is your year to get married; I feel it in my bones." Each year D., seeing this as permission and encouragement, would go forth to find a husband, finding a suitable one usually within a few months. Then the mother, afraid her daughter might actually get married and move out, would pick the man apart, finding fault with him and otherwise harassing the daughter until the daughter gave up the relationship. The loss of the relationship resulted in the daughter's acute psychosis, with feelings of loss of hope associated with fears of loss of identity and delusions of being controlled. The acute psychosis required several months of hospitalization with pharmacotherapy, individual psychotherapy, and milieu therapy.

Each time after the patient improved, the mother convinced the staff to discharge the patient home. The mother would say, "She is too sick to be out there on her own, and she has no place to go but home with us."

Of course, the mother would begin the cycle over on New Year's Day with the announcement that "D, I feel this is your year to get married." And soon the patient would once again become ill and have to be hospitalized.

Rule: Assist the patient to grow away from his or her parents when possible, using the support of a hospital during the acute illness and then a halfway house or day care, especially if there is no alternative other than to discharge the patient home. Use the halfway house or day care to place and maintain a wedge between the patient and his or her infantilizing parent.

Rule: Whenever possible take sides with the patient. Do this even when it means countermanding parents who are paying for the treatment. Tell the parents that they are paying for you to help their child get better, not to be their messenger, go-between, or tool for manipulation.

2. Double binding. The therapist, repeating an earlier pathological parental stance, issues orders impossible to follow because they are contradictory, and allows no path of escape (or, when there is one, closes it off.) The patient's retaliation is through the sword of, and the patient's escape is through the shield of, schizophrenia.

Example. In the following case the way out was through fantasy; the patient became autistic.

A patient had the following, double-binding history. His mother brought her senile mother to live with her and the patient. The patient's senile grandmother regularly told the patient, "The kidnapers are waiting for you—I see them out of the window." The child was of course too young to leave (although he tried to run away). All he could do was to beg the grandmother to stop. But she would not. So he turned to his mother for help. The mother responded with, "You are a bad person to complain so. Instead of complaining about her, you should be nicer to her. Can't you see she worries because she loves you?"

The double-binded adult schizophrenic patient feels helpless, so regresses; feels angry, so attacks him- or herself or others; feels unloved, so becomes depressed; and feels betrayed, so becomes paranoid.

3. Being overinvolved with the family, with the patient excluded. If you see the parents with the patient in family therapy, do not become overly "thick" with them. It is a temptation because they are often more intact than the patient and because they are often the ones paying. Refer out if this begins to happen. To break the tie with you, you might make the referral through a neutral third party, such as an agency.

Example. One therapist overinvolved with a male schizophrenic's mother, to the patient's consternation, granted the mother's wish, "Please don't say hello to my son because for him 'hello' means 'too much sex.' "

4. Overauthoritarianism. The regressed patient needs support and guidance, not authoritarian control. Many schizophrenics stop treatment because the ther-

apist's attitude resembles the parent's overauthoritarian attitude. Teams in an inpatient setting have a way of becoming too authoritarian, even bossy. The suggestions they give when good are undone when conveyed in a way that makes the patient feel devoured, or as one schizophrenic put it, "just like home."

5. Undermedicating. Schizophrenic patients who need medication should not be treated by psychotherapy alone.

PARANOIA

1. Joining in. The therapist sides with the patient in the patient's vendettas because they are like his or her own or because he or she admires how the patient can tell the world off.

2. Allowing the paranoid fantasies to flourish. Of course, you have to be careful to avoid crossing the paranoid patient to spare the patient's feelings, and to avoid provoking excessive anger, as happened in the following case:

A paranoid psychotherapist did consultations in a nursing home. The nursing home called for a routine consultation at 5:45, after business hours. The therapist, believing himself to be the victim of an injustice, was furious. He complained to his own therapist, "Look how badly I am treated; look how everybody takes advantage of me." The therapist responded, "It was probably an innocent error; probably they believed that your phone was in your office, and you wouldn't get the message until tomorrow." The patient responded, "Still, it's never wise to call for a routine consultation after business hours," to which his therapist responded, "Business is business, and you have to take the good with the bad." The patient, feeling crossed, exploded.

The therapist who is too careful to avoid challenging delusional beliefs avoids upsetting the patient but gives a silent blessing to delusions. The beliefs are sooner or later elaborated to include the therapist, who now becomes one of the objects of persecution in the flourishing paranoid system.

3. Treating for depression instead of for paranoia. Keep in mind the following:

a. Paranoid delusions usually contain depressive trends. For example, the patient who says, "I am persecuted," will often add, "And this makes me depressed."

b. A fall in self-esteem is present in paranoia as in depression, but in paranoia it is the result of the conviction that one is being persecuted, not, as in depression, the result of guilt.

c. Paranoid patients are usually paranoid enough to hide the paranoia. They might then emphasize the depression, perhaps just to create a false (more benign) diagnostic impression.

Example. A patient said, "I am depressed because I lost my lover." But she was not as depressed as she was paranoid. Exploration revealed that she believed herself the "special beloved of a rock star." She continued, "I am depressed because he first called me bad names over television, such as slut and whore, then abandoned me."

4. Being too personally remote. This worsens the patient's paranoia when the patient begins to wonder, I suspect he is cooking something up he isn't telling me about.

5. Failing to explain. Therapists worsen the patient's paranoia when they fail to give reassuring explanations for each and every comment they make and/or action they take. Do not be too mysterious with a paranoid patient.

6. Getting too close. This can provoke sexual panic, either heterosexual or homosexual, or anger when the patient feels his or her territory is invaded.

7. Seeming vulnerable. The overly kind therapist who does not set limits can frighten the patient who thinks: I might be able to murder and the therapist wouldn't want to, or be able to, stop me. As Frieda Fromm-Reichmann emphasizes (1960, p. 25), the realization of therapist vulnerability increases the patient's fear of his or her own hostile impulses. For similar reasons it may be wise to avoid seeing the patient in closed rooms in empty buildings after hours.

BORDERLINE STATE

1. Failing to anticipate devaluation. Just as the borderline in an overvaluing phase will overvalue the therapist, the same borderline in a devaluing phase will devalue the therapist. The therapist working with an overvaluing borderline fails to be prepared for the sudden, swift, often unanticipated devaluation that can occur in patients who have been "faithful" to treatment for years.

Therapy will be interrupted, and there may be a malpractice suit. Try to anticipate this response for the patient and ask the patient to "sit with it" when it occurs, not act out and leave treatment. Also, do not join in when the patient devalues others; with changing attitudes, the borderline may find his or her present worst enemies possible future best friends.

2. Allowing oneself to be seduced. This may be the case emotionally, even sexually. Do not rationalize that they need a real relationship and give them one in the belief that it will be a bridge back to health. Often it is the therapist, not the patient, who needs the relationship, with incorrect projective identification the basis of the judgmental error. (In projective identification the therapist assumes, without evidence, that "you are just like me.")

3. Treating the symptoms, not the disease. Transient neurotic, psychotic, and characterological symptoms are characteristic for these patients. For example, they become anxious, have micropsychotic breaks or look narcissistic, then remit spontaneously or undergo a change in disorder. Following spontaneous remission it may be inappropriate to prematurely discharge the patient from treatment and/or award oneself excessive congratulations associated with excessive self-overestimation of one's power and skill.

AFFECTIVE DISORDER—MANIA

1. Underdiagnosing. The therapist who finds the patient amusing, creative, or special may on that account fail to identify and treat affective disorder, or,

identifying the disorder, nevertheless fail to identify and treat resultant judgmental errors. In one case the therapist admired a patient's aggressive investment strategy so much that he overlooked how the patient neared bankruptcy. It is typical for the therapist to fail to identify pathological manic behavior when the behavior is responsible for a degree of social or occupational achievement.

2. Overdiagnosing. The therapist identifies normal euphoria as manic. The following rule may be helpful: Hypomanic or manic euphoria arises from a bed of anger and depression, not present in normal euphoria—for example, joy.

3. Overemphasizing organic factors. Some patients whose affective disorder is not the product of a chemical imbalance blame their pathology on chemical imbalance to avoid awareness of their thoughts and feelings. In these patients the belief that they suffer from a chemical imbalance can be a symptom—a soft grandiose delusion that says, "My chemistry is unique," or a soft paranoid delusion that says, like other paranoid delusions, "I am the way I am because of events beyond my control." Invariably, at least *some* elements in all affective disorders are emotional, not chemical (if only the personality structure). Especially to be avoided is matching patient lack of insight with therapist lack of insight, so that the therapist always responds to the patient who says, "I have no emotional problems, just chemical problems," with, "I agree; let's alter your chemistry, and overlook you as a person."

4. Subtle encouragement of pathology. Here the therapist encourages the patient's inappropriate euphoric attitudes and behaviors perhaps because the therapist's own life (sex, work) is dull and drab.

AFFECTIVE DISORDER—DEPRESSION

1. Unintended criticism. All clarifications and interpretations have a critical aspect. The patient hears, not the simple statement of dynamic fact that the therapist intends, but instead hears, This is a bad way to be, and you are bad because you are this way. The patient will respond less to the substance than to the perceived condemnation. The therapist should be careful to interpret from within the context of a fear rather than from within the context of a wish, and to apologize for each and every clarification and interpretation's critical aspects.

2. Inappropriate reassurances. Reassurances meant to comfort the patient backfire when the patient instead believes (correctly or incorrectly) the therapist does not understand and/or is oblivious to his or her plight and/or expects little from the patient. One therapist reassured his patient, depressed because of marital problems, with, "Either he comes back or he doesn't. If he does, then you have him back. If he doesn't, then you are young enough to find another man. That isn't such a bad spot to be in." But the patient heard a different message, leaving her with the impression, He doesn't understand how bad I feel and how depressing it is to be in this position. And the patient thought, He is saying this because he thinks I am not smart enough to turn things around and get my husband back.

3. Overattribution of all thought, attitude or behavior to depression. While

some therapists fail to identify as depressive equivalents such behaviors as gambling or such attitudes as loss of interest, just as common and wrong is the tendency to attribute every thought, attitude or behavior to hidden depression.

4. Excusing by invoking depression. All behavior, even the most amoral psychopathy, can, if you like, be excused as a product of depression. Sample (in this case tenuous) formulation: This patient embezzled, not for the money, but to get into trouble—to punish himself because his depression told him he was a bad person.

5. Sharing overpessimism. The therapist accepts and fails to challenge the patient's pessimistic view, for example, of the future, especially when it coincides with a pessimistic view of the therapist's own. An example is a lonely female therapist agreeing with a 54-year-old woman that she is now "too over the hill to make new friends."

6. Sharing masochism. The therapist does not challenge the patient's self-abnegating attitudes, self-deprivation, or self-torture, believing with him or her that such attitudes are admirable because they are good for the soul or are admirably moral or religious.

7. Provoking further negative therapeutic reaction. Depressed patients become more depressed when they improve, since they do not feel entitled to get better. The therapist responds by stepping up the treatment, thus making the patient even more, rather than less, depressed. (A discussion of the patient's fear of success must precede further therapy.)

8. Failing to discuss depressive transference. The therapist overlooks the patient's disappointments in therapy and in the therapist. Of course the depressed patient who is depressed because he or she expects too much will invariably become dissatisfied with treatment for the same reason.

9. Overlooking real troubles (and the reverse, overlooking dynamics). The therapist emphasizes development/dynamics while not seeing the patient's plight in the here and now. (And the reverse may be the case: the therapist overlooks dynamics and blames everything on problems in the here and now.)

10. Making the patient's procrustean bed. An example of one-size-fits-all formulations is, All depressive patients are worse in the morning. In fact many are better in the morning. This is true for patients with a reactive depression who feel like a newborn each morning when they arise, but who then become depressed as the day progresses as they find themselves beaten down by circumstances.

PASSIVE DEPENDENT PERSONALITY DISORDER

Here the precautions of treatment are as follows:

1. Failing to steer the proper course between (a) excessive therapist remoteness, with the result that the crippled passive dependent patient cannot have a needed sustaining dependent relationship, and (b) excessive therapist closeness, with the result that the patient is infantilized and prevented from growing.

2. Working with the patient even though you do not like the patient. Therapists who do not like dependent patients should admit this and not work with them. Too often they instead condemn the patient for being overly dependent or condemn themselves for keeping the patient in treatment overlong and making the patient unnecessarily dependent on therapy.

PASSIVE AGGRESSIVE PERSONALITY DISORDER

1. Being provoked. Do not react to the passive aggression by retaliating, by becoming vengeful, with retaliatory passive aggression of your own. One therapist, angry with his patient for not paying the bill, "accidentally" locked the door and kept her waiting outside for most of her session.

One elderly patient told his psychiatrist, whose office was on the third floor, "At least when I come here I get exercise climbing the steps." At another time he said that "these three flights of steps are causing me chest pain; I hope I don't have a heart attack climbing up them just to come to your office." The angry psychiatrist felt, I don't like this patient, then began to think, I don't wish to continue to see him because Medicare doesn't pay enough for psychotherapy. The therapist also found himself siding with the patient's wife against the patient, using the excuse, "You have an untreatable personality disorder." Finally, the therapist acted out by sedating the patient with benzodiazepines for his "nerves" and by cutting him down to once-a-month sessions, "Enough for monitoring your pharmacotherapy."

SADOMASOCHISTIC PERSONALITY DISORDER

Suffering and causing suffering. An example of masochistic suffering is seeing the patient at times that are inconvenient for the therapist. Eventually the therapist resents the suffering, becomes angry, then retaliates, typically in passive-aggressive, covertly sadistic, fashion. Examples of covert sadistic retaliation are hurtful "deep interpretations" or siding with the spouse against the patient. An analyst expressed covert sadism by insisting that a patient, who had a full-time job 20 miles away from the therapist's office, come for sessions at 11:00 A.M., right in the middle of the work morning. A therapist expressed covert sadism by creating financial hardship by seeing a patient one more time a week than was absolutely necessary. Still another, believing of his suicidal patient that "the world would be a better place if he *did* commit suicide," allowed that his patient's life was his own and that he was justified in taking it when and if he chose.

NARCISSISTIC PERSONALITY DISORDER

Special treatment. The narcissistic patient often requests and is given special treatment. The therapist makes exceptions and bends rules. Such special treatment is often not special but inferior—to the patient's immediate or eventual detriment. Furthermore, the narcissistic patients who convince the therapist to give them special treatment rarely appreciate the special treatment they get. Indeed, they believe the therapist a fool for falling for the ploy, the pathology of which they recognize, and believe the therapist an incompetent for not setting the limits they themselves know should have been set.

OBSESSIVE-COMPULSIVE PERSONALITY DISORDER

1. Overlooking ego-syntonicity. Many of these patients want to keep their symptoms. Not only do their symptoms reduce anxiety, but they are

a source of pride, for example the pride of perfectionism;

a source of high self-esteem, for example the high self-esteem of cleanliness;

a source of moral smugness, for example, that which results from pleasurable, excessive self-abnegation;

a source of feelings of power, for example, those that originate from a sense of being in control and in controlling others;

a source of masochistic pleasure, for example, that which originates from the self-torture of repetition;

a source of sadistic pleasure, for example, that which originates from the torture of others by withholding.

One patient believed, I am the only one in town smart enough to wear galoshes, not rubbers, when it rains; everybody else gets the bottom of his pants wet in a heavy rain and has to spend the money to take them to the cleaners. Another was ecstatic for minutes after he found and corrected a grammatical error of his therapist. A third took pleasure in "being able to resist that delicious cocktail I have every night."

2. Excessive neutrality. This has unfavorable consequences when the uncertain obsessional in a paralytic bind depends on the therapist to move him or her forward and becomes anxious when the therapist is not forthcoming. For this reason, at least in the beginning, it is the more active, even more opinionated therapist, who may do better with these patients.

3. Impatience. The therapist might handle loss of patience with a repetitive obsessional by issuing orders that are difficult to follow, and secretly meant to be critical.

For example, a patient had a vinegar sediment compulsion. He searched through one bottle after another to find "the one with the least sediment." He was told, "You better not do that otherwise the people will see you and find you peculiar. You may even attract the attention of the supermarket manager, who may believe that you are up to something illegal and call the police." The patient, now feeling defective, felt compelled to repair the defect. He did this symbolically—by trying to purchase the purest bottle of vinegar he could find. And so the checking ritual got worse, instead of better.

HYSTERICAL DISORDERS

1. Failure to dispel positive Oedipal—(but see the disclaimer below) transference when a resistance. The therapist fails to appreciate how the positive transference is as much a resistance at times as the negative. He or she thinks, We are getting along well, when in fact the patient is being seductive to avoid getting treatment. A typical result is that the patient improves, not because therapy is effective, but because improvement is part of the seduction of the therapist. This is a transference cure, barely better than no cure at all because it is usually unsustainable for very long. There is a relapse when the therapist disappoints the patient, for example, by remaining more personally distant than the patient would like. Symptoms return, often as part of a symbolic castration, with the hidden message, I render you defective to retaliate for your ignoring me.

2. Overemphasis on the sexual aspects of the positive transference. There are a number of aspects of positive Oedipus (but see the disclaimer below), and thus a number of different elements composing the positive transference. For example, some patients do not want to *seduce* the therapist so much as they want to *manipulate* the therapist into siding with them against a rival, often a latter-day version of the parent of the same sex.

3. Overuse of dynamic approaches. Our ability to understand the dynamics in the hysteric tempts us to overuse dynamic approaches for treatment. But remember the following principle: Treatment does not always depend on cause. (As an example, the treatment of a delusion may be with phenothiazines even though the cause of the delusion is not "phenothiazine deficiency.")

Disclaimer: There are many viable theories of hysteria. The therapist who is not enamored of the analytic-Oedipal explanation or approach should explain or approach the problem in other ways. For example, the therapist might treat using advice, suggestion, or hypnosis.

Example. One hysterical patient devalued any available man by a process that seemed akin to psychological castration. Brief Oedipal analysis was not helpful. Very effective, however, was the warning, "You aren't getting any younger, and you don't want to be alone. So don't devalue that man; try to see his many good points. He's not perfect, but he's good enough."

ANXIETY DISORDER

1. Extremism of theoretical position. Some therapists who believe that anxiety is thoughtless, that is, purely physiological, overlook the psychological basis of anxiety. Others, believing that all anxiety is psychological, overlook the organic causes or sequelae of anxiety.

2. Misemphasis of dynamics. Of those therapists who believe that anxiety has a psychological cause, some emphasize the sexual while ignoring the hostile, or vice versa.

3. Misuse of drugs. Mistreatment comes in two opposite forms: addicting the patient unnecessarily to benzodiazepines or using psychological approaches when pharmacological approaches are more efficient and effective.

PHOBIA

1. Treating only the phobia in the patient, but not the patient with the phobia.

a. Overlooking the psychological. As with anxiety, phobia has a psychological as well as a biological basis. The therapist who overlooks the psychological (defensive) meaning of a phobia may treat his or her patient's symptom but not really the patient's problem.

b. Treating all phobias as "created equal." Even though they are both phobias, simple logic would dictate that a "social" phobia—for example, a fear of being seen urinating in the men's room—has a different psychological basis from an agoraphobia—for example, the inability to leave the house without hanging on the arm of mother or another companion.

2. Confusing normal with phobic. Simple logic would dictate that a fear of "creepy, crawly things" or a fear of screwing in a light bulb (because the bulb might pop) is so universal that it is hardly phobic.

PSYCHOPATHIC/ANTISOCIAL PERSONALITY DISORDER

There are seven deadly sins:

1. The therapist gets the patient out of trouble when the patient deserves to get into trouble.

2. The therapist gets the patient out of trouble when in the long run it might be better to let the patient take the consequences and learn from them.

3. The therapist treats a concocted illness as if it were legitimate. There are essentially two classes of such "concocted" illness: Munchausen's-like illness (DSM-III-R factitious disorder with physical symptoms), where the concocted illness is physical, and Ganser's-like illness (DSM-III-R factitious disorder with psychological symptoms), where the concocted illness is psychological. (In the category of Ganser's may be included such hysterical hallucinations as, "Animals are biting me." Characteristic of this and other hysterical hallucinations is that they tell a simple, childlike story.) The following examples are of a factitious disorder with psychological symptoms:

An embezzler concocted the symptom of an obsession with the number three to convince his therapist that his embezzlement was not criminal, "because a product of an uncontrollable obsession with numbers. The reason I take money is so that my checking account balance can be made to read all 3s."

Another therapist failed to see how a patient initially believed to be suffering from stress disorder was malingering to maintain compensation. (Often the illness is part real, part malingered, so the problem is more one of overemphasis or underemphasis.)

4. The therapist believes a patient's self-serving story without checking, for example, hearing the other side or finding out the facts.

5. The therapist covertly encourages or fails to discourage antisocial behavior in the patient out of secret rebelliousness or iconoclasm of his or her own.

6. The therapist him- or herself behaves in a psychopathic or antisocial fashion. Lying on insurance forms or cutting time short shows the patient, not how to cure, but how to maintain his or her illness.

7. The therapist recommends group treatment to "pool rudimentary super-egos" but instead creates a pool of ids resulting in group antisocial behavior. (This often happens spontaneously to the hapless staff on an inpatient unit.)

REFERENCE

Fromm-Reichmann, Frieda. *Principles of Intensive Psychotherapy*. Chicago: The University of Chicago Press, 1960.

Part II
Special Situations

Chapter 16

Treating Schizophrenia

While some therapists believe that patients in one diagnostic category, for example schizophrenia, require treatment different from patients in another diagnostic category—psychopathy, for example—others do not tailor treatment to diagnosis.

Therapists who do not tailor treatment to diagnosis can be divided into two categories:

1. Those who make a diagnosis but treat all patients more or less alike regardless of diagnosis. Among these are the therapists who overuse such forms of treatment as psychoanalysis, insight-oriented psychotherapy, certain drugs, or some behavior therapies such as biofeedback. Treatment may be appropriate though excessive, as when a mild phobia, treatable with conditioning therapies, is instead treated in long-term psychotherapy; or it may be appropriate but not enough, as when a severe obsessional neurosis is treated only with "stop thought" therapy.

2. Those who do not make a diagnosis. They might believe, Diagnosis is not appropriate where emotional illness is concerned, or, Since diagnosis does not determine treatment, why make one.

Of course, diagnosis is not the only factor that helps us decide on a course of treatment. But it is often *one* such factor. Knowing a patient is schizophrenic, or manic, can help decide treatment, if only because it tells us what might be contraindicated. But we also have to know other things: How severe is the illness? Is it active or in remission? What is the family like, for example, will they support the patient if he or she temporarily gets worse before getting better? What does the patient want—does he or she want medication, or would he or she prefer to "sweat out therapy" instead?

In the following chapter we explore some modifications to be made in the treatment of schizophrenia.

SCHIZOPHRENIA

The special problems of the schizophrenic—and relevant tasks for the therapist treating schizophrenia—may be divided into two groups—general (problems for all schizophrenics) and specific (problems that tend to be characteristic of a specific subtype of schizophrenia).

General

1. Dereism, autism, and related phenomena. The term *dereism* seems less mysterious when hyphenated to become "de-reism" and when we realize that "re-ism" is related to "re-ality."

The dereistic patient is one who is isolated, divorced from reality because of self-preoccupation, narcissism, disinterest, or inability to concentrate on external matters. One aspect of being so divorced is the inability to reality test, to differentiate what *is* so from what is *believed* to be so.

The term *autism* also looks mysterious until we realize it contains the prefix *auto,* meaning "self." Essentially, *autism* means "self-ism."

Autism generally refers to self-preoccupation. The patient might be self-preoccupied for some of the same reasons that he or she might be dereistic.

What is the relationship between autism and such familiar symptoms as delusions and hallucinations? There are two possibilities: (1) Some believe that the isolation resulting from autism is responsible for symptoms such as delusions and hallucinations through a mechanism akin to sensory deprivation (Federn, 1957). (2) Others believe instead that preoccupation with delusions and hallucinations is responsible for the isolation of autism.

Dereism and autism may be inherent (genetic) and/or developed, originating, for example, in pathological overdependence of a child on a parent, or, if a parent, in pathological overdependence on a child. (This "stay at home" isolation, from the schizophrenic spectrum, must be distinguished from such other isolation as phobic, due to fear, and depressive, due to low self-esteem.)

A conservative approach to treating the unreality, self-preoccupation, and oft-associated delusions and hallucinations is long-term, problem-solving psychotherapy. In this form of psychotherapy the therapist discusses, not development or dynamics, but the here and now. This avoids uncovering frightening, guilty thoughts and feelings, thereby making the patient anxious. Only experienced, devoted, talented, available therapists should use anything like Elvin Semrad's technique (personal communication) of placing his hand over his heart then asking the schizophrenic patient, "Where is the pain in your heart?" Emphasize such educative techniques as the giving of advice and reality testing. Encourage the patient to try—to practice relating as much as possible. Develop a trusting relationship with the patient and help the patient, if an inpatient, develop a trusting relationship with the therapeutic team. Use the trusting relationship as a fulcrum to help the patient abandon his or her schizophrenic isolation and begin to relate to others. You will be tested. The patient will try to provoke you to reject him or her. And you will fail the test. The important thing is, not whether you fail or not, but whether you try again after failing. Tell the patient you failed the test because it was too difficult to pass. Ask him or her to make the next test a little easier; and say that in exchange you will try a little harder the next time. Avoid being provoked into rejecting the patient.

Group (with leader or self-help) and activity therapy (e.g., horticultural therapy) are helpful. In activity therapy the relationship with the therapist helps as well as the activity itself.

A certain amount of isolation should be accepted, and the patient encouraged to make the best of it. The patient might be encouraged to take a job where he or she can remain isolated from others, for example, in a pet shop, or in the post-office sorting room. To be avoided is excessive pressure to relate, especially attempts to force the patient against his or her will into active human intercourse, no matter how much the patient complains of his or her isolation. Forcing the patient to resocialize is not only doomed to failure but counterproductive because it makes the patient angry with the therapist and increases stubbornness and negativism.

Delusions and hallucinations require special treatment. The therapist may treat a paranoid or grandiose formation verbally using the technique of Frieda Fromm-Reichmann (1960, 175), who recommended that the psychiatrist should not argue about hallucinations and delusions but instead state quite simply and clearly that he or she does not see or hear what the patient professes to see or hear. Follow this by trying to interest the patient in the investigation of why he or she sees and hears what the psychiatrist does not. While there are no fixed rules, antipsychotic medication (e.g., phenothiazines) is indicated both for paranoid delusions and hallucinations and for grandiose delusions and hallucinations when part of the schizophrenic process and not primarily the result of an affective disorder. The use of lithium as an antischizophrenic medication is controversial.

To be avoided are simplistic confrontational techniques intended to force the dereistic patient to face reality. A legendary example is the doctor who showed a patient an X ray of her throat to get her to see that there was no cat stuck in her throat. Such concrete, simplistic approaches are sometimes met by sullenness or psychotic rationalization. ("That must be the wrong X ray".) Simple explanations work only when the delusion is transient, as in the following case:

A patient complained about his neighbor's dog because it had been let off the leash. The neighbor responded, "I'll take that leash and ram you with it in the mouth." The patient's own dog subsequently became ill. For a few minutes the patient believed, for no real reason, that the neighbor had poisoned it to retaliate.

2. Low self-esteem. Low self-esteem is different in the schizophrenic from low self-esteem in the depressed patient. In the schizophrenic, low self-esteem is the product of a paranoid attitude toward oneself—a kind of self-persecution. Accordingly, treat low self-esteem as you treat other delusions—by administering medication or focusing on reality.

3. Flooding. This may result from an inability to filter (repress) internal perceptions and an inability to filter (ignore) external perceptions. One patient unable to filter internal perceptions could not shop because each time he considered an item, he heard conflicting commercial jingles in his head. An inability to ignore external perceptions leaves the patient overwhelmed and unable to differentiate important from unimportant. Such thought disorder as overinclusiveness and disorganization may result.

Simplification of the environment helps in two ways: arousal is diminished, allowing healing repression, and confusion is minimized, allowing organization of thought. It follows that many patients enjoy rather than resent the seclusion room. (Try this: go into the seclusion room when you feel anxious or agitated, and see if it will work for you, too.) One schizophrenic patient created the effect of autoseclusion by taking naps, not because he was sleepy, but because this way he could "detach." Other methods can be employed to reduce internal and external overstimulation. For example, in family therapy exhort or advise the parents to treat the patient in a predictable fashion, establishing a routine. (Even such controversial therapies as allergy-free environmental treatment may work not for the reasons given but because they simplify the patient's environment and so are restful.)

To be avoided are total push therapies that create flooding by pushing the patient to do tasks that are too complex or overwhelming. Double-binding the schizophrenic (discussed elsewhere) produces its disastrous effect in part by confusing him or her. Too much input by too many therapists, especially when all have different ideas (a typical complication of badly done milieu therapy) also floods and agitates the patient.

4. Infantilism. We call schizophrenics immature, even infantile, because of the following traits:

a. They think like children, for example, concretely (literally). An example of blurring the distinction between abstract and concrete is found in the patient who believed his therapist intended to give him the message, "You are trash," by putting a trash basket next to his chair.

b. They relate like children, relating, for example, to only a part of an object, such as its warmth-giving qualities.

c. They use defenses that are regressive, rendering them helpless, like children. The defenses they use typically interfere with, more than they promote, function (for example, regression rather than reaction formation).

The therapist's task becomes that of diminishing the hold of the child over the adult. The therapist may encourage maturity through such techniques as resocialization, group therapy (peer pressure), or the giving of rewards for adult behavior (token economy).

Always respect the child in the patient. Never pressure the patient to do adult tasks he or she finds impossible. This makes the patient anxious, thereby promoting further regression. Some individual therapists and teams, in their overzealousness, put unbearable pressure on the patient to be more adult—to socialize, get married, and/or relate to his or her parents. At the same time they paradoxically fail to respect the adult in the patients. They fail to consult the patients' wishes, believing that since they are schizophrenic, they are not allowed, because of being too sick, to have a say in their own future.

5. Primary and secondary anhedonia. By *primary anhedonia* is meant an innate inability to experience pleasure, perhaps in-born. By *secondary anhedonia* is meant a developed inability to experience pleasure, perhaps due to fear, perhaps the result of guilt.

Primary anhedonia is difficult to treat because few therapists find a way to create something not already there. The therapist who treats secondary anhedonia does so in one of two ways: directly, by exhortation, and indirectly, by acknowledging guilt and then employing the guilt-diminishing techniques described throughout. These techniques are useful for schizophrenic as well as nonschizophrenic patients, except for the cautionary suggestions listed below.

Heed these warnings when treating anhedonia:

In treating primary anhedonia, accept the schizophrenic patient's limitations. The psychotherapist who insists the anhedonic patient "think enjoyable thoughts and do enjoyable things" is no different from the speech therapist who orders the aphasic patient to name an object he or she cannot name. In addition, ordering a patient to do that which he or she is incapable of doing makes you demanding, unrealistic, and/or punitive. You frustrate the patient, intimidate the patient, make him or her angry, make him or her feel helpless, promote projection of anger (paranoia toward the therapist), and encourage defensive regression. One schizophrenic may have been driven to suicide by the therapist's forcing upon him a list of "pleasant thoughts to have when depressed"—none of which he was able to have let alone sustain. The list suggested "thoughts about green meadows; thoughts about your love for your pet. . . . "

In treating secondary anhedonia, proceed slowly to avoid overpermissiveness with flooding, and proceed selectively, allowing some guilt to remain, and where appropriate, balancing guilt reduction with guilt promotion.

A rule to follow is this: While selectively decreasing guilt is useful for the more obsessive and more paranoid schizophrenic patient, increasing guilt is a technique more useful for the impulsive schizophrenic patient.

6. Unhealthy defenses. Schizophrenic patients overuse not only the unhealthy defenses of regression (as above) but also projection and denial.

To treat, replace unhealthy defenses with defenses and defensive processes less unhealthy, such as the following:

a. Obsessive organization. The therapist who gives the schizophrenic patient simple repetitive tasks that *do not insult his or her intelligence* helps promote healthy obsessionalism (to counteract unhealthy disorganization).

b. Reaction formation. Encourage asexuality in some patients, for example, the patient flooded by guilty homosexual wishes. Encourage excessive loving in some patients, for example being charitable to replace excessive hating, for example being paranoid.

c. Repression. As an example of a success story, one patient after improving could not remember any of his delusions. The entire period of acute psychosis was referred to as "that time when I slept a lot."

d. Phobic defenses (such as homophobia). These can replace projective defenses (such as the delusion of being called queer). (Here what is sometimes better for the patient is, alas, sometimes worse for society.)

7. Excessively strong superego. The defense of projection, creating paranoid delusions, often occurs at the behest of a punitive conscience.

In treatment, soften an excessively punitive conscience by the mechanisms outlined throughout.

8. Excessively weak superego. In treatment, harden an excessively permissive conscience by the mechanisms outlined throughout, when the patient is impulsive and/or psychopathic.

Caution: Avoid guilt-increasing techniques that rely on fiat or mandate originating from inappropriate therapist morality. These promote isolation by increasing inappropriate guilt. An example is conveying to the patient the therapist's own feelings that one's body is dirty. Also to be avoided are guilt-increasing techniques that are really unwanted side effects of inflaming forbidden instincts. An example is guilt provoked by a therapist who teases a patient sexually, thereby awakening unwanted, forbidden, latent homosexual feelings.

9. Pseudoneurotic or pseudocharacterological aspects. Many schizophrenics have neurotic, or characterological symptoms. They have them because the schizophrenic process is selective. It leaves the patient with the ego strength to resolve conflict in the same way that it is resolved in the neurotic or personality-disordered patient (i.e., with neurotic or characterological symptoms). (Others only *appear* to have them. Delusions may be misdiagnosed, as when the fear of meeting one's persecutors outdoors is misdiagnosed as agoraphobia, or when delusional suspiciousness is misdiagnosed as avoidant personality disorder.)

There are three rules to keep in mind:

a. Encourage more of what normal function is present. All, or almost all, schizophrenic patients maintain the ability to function normally in one or more ways. As examples, the delusional paranoid patients at times hearing voices are at other times free of voices. Their voices might appear intermittently, for example, only under stress, being suppressed at other, perhaps less stressful times. One schizophrenic patient hearing voices was able to function as a flight controller in a busy airport until, with increasing illness, he found the voices contaminating the messages he received from the planes.

b. Do not treat schizophrenic symptoms as if they were neurotic or characterological. Interpretations the patient cannot tolerate will arouse anxiety that can be dealt with only by such heroic defenses as regression. These include interpretations from the side of the wish, not the fear; interpretations about forbidden sexual wishes; Oedipal interpretations though accurate; and transference interpretations that arouse intolerable passions toward a therapist highly charged with feelings—a person more significant for the patient than many therapists believe. Here especially the therapist should avoid what Avery Weisman once semihumorously called deep therapy. He defined *deep therapy* for his present purposes as therapy in which the therapist (and by extension the patient) is "in over his or her head."

c. A patient should be treated with caution when using uncovering therapy until schizophrenia is ruled out. Only the "safer" techniques should be used if schizophrenia is suspected. These safer techniques include environmental manipulation, encouragement of identification with strengths in the therapist, exhortation, corrective emotional experience, and family therapy when directed at removing stress rather than at resolving conflict—for example, encouraging mutual respect rather than making Oedipal interpretations.

Specific Subsyndromes

Paranoid schizophrenia

DIAGNOSIS

1. Avoid misdiagnosing from the overattribution of significance to the *grandiose* element found in all paranoid delusions. This leads to the misdiagnosis of mania. All paranoid delusions are grandiose because all suggest that the patient is the central figure of a persecutory scheme. But this is paranoid grandiosity, not manic grandiosity. (In manic grandiosity the patient believes, not, I am important because I am specially persecuted, but rather, I am important because I am specially wonderful.)

2. Avoid misdiagnosing from the overattribution of significance to the *depressive* element found in all paranoid delusions. This leads to the misdiagnosis of depression. The paranoid patient is often misdiagnosed as depressed when he or she says, "I am blue because I am being persecuted." Really depressed patients are blue, not because they feel persecuted, but because they feel worthless. Hint: In the paranoid schizophrenic patient, affect is often blunted, or flattened. Any depression or euphoria has a constricted, remote, two-dimensional quality. Especially dangerous here is the use of antidepressant drugs alone (i.e., without covering agents such as phenothiazines).

TREATMENT

Pathological projection/delusions/hallucinations. In all projection, normal and pathological, the patient defensively disavows a wish or a feeling, for example, a sense of guilt, by attributing it to others. While the defense relieves anxiety and guilt, it creates as many problems as it solves:

a. Anxiety is replaced by fear. Anxiety about a forbidden personal motivation is replaced by fear—of the same forbidden personal motivation, only now attributed to another and directed toward the patient. The patient who believed his therapist called him trash did so in part to avoid awareness of his own angry, demeaning feelings about his therapist.

b. Reality is distorted. This naturally follows upon the patient's reading the motives of others according to his or her own motives. When the "perhaps" drops out ("perhaps you are after me"), delusions appear. The patient might be convinced that he or she is being persecuted, criticized, or demeaned (delusions), and may even begin to hallucinate (to hear, see, smell, taste, or feel something that is not there).

c. The patient hates others. This happens when hostile attitudes toward the self become hostile attitudes toward others.

Recommended approaches are as follows: treating the distortion of reality. Teach the patient about the process of projection. Even with the disorganized schizophrenic, "knowledge is power." The therapist might say, "You are falsely empathic, attributing your own wishes, fears, and so on, to others who may not be similarly inclined. Invariably what you do is elaborate a grain of truth in others with pounds of distortion of your own, then insist you are all correct when in fact you are only partly correct." Remind the patient of the expression, It takes one to know one.

HIDING THE PROBLEM

1. You might "allow" the patient to keep the delusions or hallucinations if only he or she will be so good as to hide them from public scrutiny. Ask the patient not to act on delusions or to talk back to hallucinations. One patient was permitted a pass from the hospital to attend a symphony, with the only proviso that he would not talk to his voices while the orchestra was playing.

Approaches not recommended are as follows:

a. Reality testing that amounts to arguing with the patient ("That just isn't so"). Resist this. Delusions and hallucinations, like other symptoms, are defensive, and thus needed. A typical consequence of challenging the delusion too early or too much is the incorporation of the therapist into the delusional system. The patient now thinks, You hate me just like all the others. The result may be termination of therapy by the patient and/or assault upon the therapist.

b. Heroic, especially when silly, techniques such as the above-described use of a personal stereo to counteract voices or the above-described use of a list of pleasant things to think about. These methods are contraindicated because the patient is brighter than we give him or her credit for being and often perceives the therapist's approach as unsophisticated, if not unintelligent.

c. Treating delusions or hallucinations as if they were a sin.

d. Overtreatment of delusions or hallucinations even when they are compatible with good function: removing them no matter what the cost.

e. Being overly kind. Sullivan (1954) suggested that the therapist be faintly unpleasant to the paranoid patient. While hostility to one's patients is not recommended, even though faint, the recommendation is based on a sound principle: The overly kind and loving therapist typically threatens the paranoid patient. The kindness has a paradoxical, often dangerous effect when the therapist is perceived as seductive and/or excessively permissive.

f. Sneering. This is contraindicated for all patients, but especially for those who are paranoid. One way to sneer is to ask the covertly hostile question, Why do you think you are special enough to be the target of computer messages? This merely belittles the patient and so reduces his or her self-esteem.

2. Thought disorder. Some paranoid schizophrenics have the following thought disorders:

a. Loosening of associations, sometimes word salad: characterized by disorganized, even incomprehensible, thinking.

b. Blocking, often characterized by an inability to think because thoughts seem plucked from the patient's head.

c. Tangentiality and circumstantiality—wandering away from (tangentiality) or talking around (circumstantiality) the point. These can be innate or, incredible though it may sound, purposeful and meaningful, for example, manifestation of paranoid evasiveness. (Not all tangentiality/circumstantiality is a manifestation of paranoia. Obsessive-compulsive patients can also be tangential and/or circumstantial due to stubborn withholding of a point the patient knows we are waiting to hear.)

Recommended approaches include the following:

a. Resolving the underlying problem when the thought disorder is purposeful or motivated. If the thought disorder has an interpersonal aspect, if the disorganization is purposeful, perhaps to maintain distance from others, the thought disorder is potentially controllable. In other words, patients who create thought disorder for a purpose can also remain asymptomatic for a purpose. They can abandon thought disorder for the purpose of a therapy session. One hospitalized patient in whom thought disorder was motivated, and who used remoteness and incomprehensibility as a form of angry punishment and avoidance of others, was told that the therapist would return to see the patient when the patient had put his thoughts together, but not before. This behavioral "manipulation" bypassed the patient's sadomasochistic use of thought disorder.

Other thought disorder, for example, some disorganization, is the product of strong emotion, such as anger. Such disorganization may be modifiable by drugs, for example phenothiazines.

b. Hiding the problem when the thought disorder is unmodifiable. The patient with an intractable thought disorder may be asked to develop techniques for hiding his or her problem. The therapist might ask the patient with a thought disorder not to speak in a disorganized fashion in public or to remain silent until the anger that disorganizes thinking passes.

Rule: Try to avoid permitting the patient to speak in a disorganized fashion in treatment or be circumstantial while you, pained, bored, or restless, listen to unlistenable material in the belief that you are hearing revelations from the unconscious.

Rule: Short, frequent sessions may be better than long, infrequent ones for the patient who is unable to abandon his or her thought disorder for the duration of a 45–minute therapy session.

Schizoaffective schizophrenia

DIAGNOSIS

1. We see *coalesced* paranoid and affective trends, as follows:

a. Paranoid delusions and hallucinations may have an affective tone—for example, delusions and hallucinations of persecution may be of persecution of the bad self. (Note: In paranoid delusions and hallucinations without an affective tone, fantasies of persecution are often of the innocent self by malevolent beings, i.e., of the good self by the bad other.)

b. Changes in mood (i.e., euphoria and depression) may have a bizarre tinge, so that the patient feels *peculiarly* high, or *mysteriously* depressed.

c. Euphoria and depression may have fuller depth and amplitude in the schizoaffective patient than in the schizophrenic patient, in whom affect is often blunted, or flat.

2. We may see the following affective manifestations side by side with the schizophrenic:

a. Grandiose delusions and hallucinations. These may be of excessive accomplishment, or they may be erotomanic (the false belief that one is loved, often by someone famous and important).

b. Depressive delusions and hallucinations. These may be of poverty.

c. Somatic delusions and hallucinations. These may be of illness or of bodily decay.

TREATMENT

The recommended approach is as follows:

Treat paranoid, grandiose, and depressive trends in much the same way you would in the "purer" syndromes of paranoia, mania, and depression. It follows that because the schizoaffective syndrome is a "combination" syndrome, combination therapy may be required. For example, some patients require treatment with phenothiazines for paranoia, lithium for mood disorder, and an antidepressant for depression.

The approach not recommended is as follows:

Challenging the schizoaffective patient's grandiosity is not advised because the schizoaffective patient is also depressed and paranoid. Implying to such a patient that the entire FBI might not be after a nobody like him or her may reduce the grandiosity but will certainly increase the depression and paranoia.

Catatonic schizophrenia

DIAGNOSIS

The following is a typical case:

A young man went out drinking with his buddies, got too physically close when eight of them packed into a car after the bars closed, became aware of alarming homosexual feelings, and became excited because he delusionally believed he was being entrapped by the police. Then he became withdrawn and rigid. The rigidity both protected him from doing forbidden things and protected him from assault from without, as he later said, "like an animal who won't be seen and attacked if it doesn't move."

Dynamically, both excited and stuporous catatonia can be symptomatic expressions of underlying homosexual panic.

Differentiate stuporous catatonia from severely retarded depression, in which the withdrawal and immobility represent, not a means of controlling assaultiveness or a way of protecting oneself from an external assault but an expression of self-hate so great that the patient stops eating and wastes away because he or she wants to be, and so acts, dead.

TREATMENT

Recommended approaches comprise the following:

The excited hyperactive patient may exhaust him- or herself and/or become *assaultive*. Treat first with such somatic treatment as medication or ECT (only a few ECTs may be required).

The seemingly withdrawn catatonic patient may hear, be responsive to, and remember everything we say. There are two rules that follow:

1. The patient is listening, so never say things in front of the patient you do not want him or her to hear. The assumption that the withdrawn patient is not attentive has encouraged therapists to talk about the patient in an unfavorable, critical, or snide manner. The patient hears us, resents us, and is angered with us. Complications: We may precipitate excited catatonia; at the very least, the patient remembers and resents our behavior after the acute episode is over.

2. The attentive patient will hear things you *do* want the patient to hear. You may make certain diagnostic assumptions and begin a form of one-way psychotherapy. You can, for example, reassure the patient who feels guilty about homosexuality that it is possible to have homosexual feelings without being a homosexual, sympathize with and understand his or her anger, enhance self-esteem. (In the hospital on rounds, a few minutes of musing aloud upon these topics can help produce remission.)

Physical care is important, for the patient may neglect proper nutrition, have to be fed (either by hand or by tube), and in time (should the illness become chronic) develop decubiti or contractures without proper nursing care.

Where remission does not occur spontaneously or follow supportive or interpretative psychotherapy, phenothiazines may be helpful (especially when delusions or hallucinations cause the catatonic withdrawal). Here, too, a short course of ECT can produce rapid remission. (This may be more effective for patients with an underlying affective disorder than for those who are basically paranoid.)

Undifferentiated schizophrenia

DIAGNOSIS

Undifferentiated schizophrenics have multiple and extensive but transient and poorly formed symptoms. One patient had transient fragmentary paranoid delusions associated with transient fragmentary erotomanic delusions, as well as transient fragmentary garbled hallucinations (of murmuring).

TREATMENT

The recommended approach is as follows:

Multiple symptom-oriented approaches are indicated. Drugs, psychotherapy, and behavioral therapy might be combined. There are two reasons for this: (1) different symptoms require different approaches and (2) treatment for one problem can make another problem worse. Example: phenothiazines given for hallucinations increase anhedonia, requiring total push behavioral intervention.

Because pathology is extensive, usurps conflict-free ego, and creates severe illness unmodified by strengths, the patient may often have to be hospitalized and rehabilitated as if he or she were a child—for example, taught how to manage his or her life and helped with the simplest activities of daily living.

The approach not recommended is as follows:

Overinterpreting, misapplying analytic principles, and so on. Parenthetically, these patients are so sick that few therapists are tempted to cause harm by being overzealous.

Disorganized hebephrenic (regressive) schizophrenia

DIAGNOSIS

These patients are primarily regressed: inappropriate, infantile, and unable to care for themselves.

TREATMENT

The recommended approach is as follows:

The patients have so few strengths that they often have to be institutionalized, with their basic care assumed by others.

Basic care-giving, often long-term, is the cornerstone of treatment. Some therapists try pharmacologic agents such as the phenothiazines. In practice these are often used less for their effect on target symptoms (such as paranoia and catatonia, which tend to be poorly developed) than for behavioral "control"— that is tranquilization, including control of agitation, impulsivity, sexual or hostile acting-out, bizarreness, and primitive behaviors such as soiling.

The approach not recommended is as follows:

Some therapists, when they find that ECT and pharmacotherapy is ineffective in the recommended dose range, give higher and higher doses. While no more effective, these higher doses create unpleasant or dangerous side effects. One patient who was treated with 150 ECTs said, "Now I cannot function, and I still hear the voices from Mars."

REFERENCES

Federn, Paul. *Ego Psychology and the Psychoses*. New York: Columbia University Press, 1952.

Fromm-Reichmann, Frieda. *Principles of Intensive Psychotherapy*. Chicago: The University of Chicago Press, 1960.

Modell, Arnold H. Primitive object relationships and the predisposition to schizophrenia. *Int. J. Psychoanal.* 44: 282 91 (1963).

Sullivan, Harry Stack. *The Psychiatric Interview*. New York: W. W. Norton, 1954, p. 132.

Chapter 17

Treating Adolescent, Middle-aged, and Geriatric Patients

Treatment of adolescent, middle-aged, and geriatric patients presents special problems. Some of these special problems are presented along with recommended solutions.

TREATING THE ADOLESCENT

Adolescent Characteristics

Adolescents are

1. young. They are emotionally still children and legally still dependent on their parents.

2. transitional. They are unsettled. They are changing rapidly. Many problems are as likely to be mastered and disappear as to persist. Many symptoms are as likely to be an interim compromise as a permanent position statement or solution.

3. action-oriented. They are a cauldron of instincts pressing for, and achieving, direct expression. Some are more contemplative than others, but most act up and many act out.

4. cocky. They are rash. They believe themselves invincible and immortal.

5. sensitive. Their feelings are so new, so strong, and so unintegrated that sometimes it seems as if everything touches a nerve.

Diagnostic Implications of Adolescent Characteristics

1. Malignant-appearing symptoms in the adolescent (e.g., symptoms that look schizophrenic or depressive) often turn out to be relatively benign.

2. The acting-out disorders (e.g, conduct disorders of adolescence) seem to predominate over the contemplative disorders (e.g., the obsessive-compulsive disorder), although early-onset contemplative adult disorders do appear.

Treatment Implications of Adolescent Characteristics

1. Two of the therapist's jobs are keeping the acting-out patient out of trouble, for example, with the law, and treating an illness in its early stages to prevent it from becoming chronic.

2. Rarely is adolescent illness completely internalized. So, families and social agencies will often have to be involved. Hint: When dealing with families, make sure that the parents are not getting the adolescent patient to act out their own emotional problems. For example, the adolescent who rides around in a car yelling obscenities may be expressing his or her parents', as much as his or her own, hostilities.

Some organic therapies (high doses of some drugs, some ECT) are inappropriate, even amoral, for use in the tender, sensitive adolescent.

TREATING THE MIDDLE-AGED PATIENT

Middle-age Crisis

This consists of at least two components: anxiety and affective.

Anxiety aspects

1. Hostile and sexual instincts can be especially threatening to the middle-aged individual because of being inimical to social position and responsibilities most have to maintain.

2. A newly intense awareness of mortality and a heretofore suppressed fear of death is also anxiety-provoking.

Affective aspects

DEPRESSION

1. Reactive depression. This may be due to the following:

a. Losses, both real and symbolic, often simultaneous: the death of parents, the "loss" of children who marry or move, and the loss of longtime friends who, after 20 or 25 years, abandon interest in the relationship, often because of a middle-age crisis of their own.

b. Awareness of physical and mental involution. Early signs of physical deterioration might be the appearance of wrinkles, or early signs of mental deterioration might be the inability to think of words, or, important for one patient, a diminution in the ability to quickly identify familiar pieces of classical music.

2. Anticipatory depression. This can be a way of preparing for the worst. Much as one patient waiting for a biopsy report convinced herself that it was cancer—"to prepare for the worst and avoid disappointment"—the middle-aged patient accustoms him- or herself to dying and death in advance to avoid unpleasant surprises later. He or she actively courts disaster, in fantasy, to avoid being its passive victim, in reality.

HYPOMANIA

Reactive hypomania is often due to denial of such depressive concerns as aging, dying, and death. In the hypomanic state individuals may act up by doing something inappropriate, such as leaving a good marriage or a good job, often on a flimsy pretext. They deny the possibility of physical deterioration by failing to have preventive checkups or by overlooking medical problems even when obvious.

Treatment Approaches to Middle-age Crisis

The middle-aged patient in middle-age crisis often requires advice as to the following:

Physical well-being

The patient should be urged to maintain his or her physical as well as emotional health. Regular checkups, good diet, and exercise can prevent and treat physical illness. The feeling of well-being that results from good diet and strenuous exercise helps anxious and depressed patients feel better. One such patient "got more relief from riding an exercise bike than all the therapy in the world."

Mental well-being

1. Dissuade some patients, particularly obsessionals and depressed patients who are better off when they keep busy and whose self-esteem depends on their work, from taking an early retirement.

2. Dissuade the patient from inappropriate attempts at achieving perpetual youth (inappropriate job changes, extramarital affairs).

3. Prepare the patient for the emotional problems of aging and for eventual death. Help him or her squirrel away relationships, interests, and so on, for the long winter ahead.

Financial well-being

Counsel about such realistic matters as money for retirement. Remember that the middle-aged patient who is scared becomes prey for the unscrupulous financial adviser no less than the elderly patient who is overwhelmed, weak, confused, and helpless.

There are special difficulties and advantages in treating the middle-aged patient, as follows:

On the negative side, the therapist if younger may not have the patient's wisdom, and it may be difficult for the younger therapist to appreciate the middle-aged patient's existential plight. (Often the patient can teach the therapist as much about that as he or she can learn from the therapist.) On the positive side, lack of wisdom may be supplanted by the therapist's youth, with which the older patient can identify—and now continue to feel young.

TREATING THE GERIATRIC PATIENT

Diagnostic Problems

General

These consist of at least three prejudices:

1. against making a neurotic, psychotic, or personality disorder diagnosis in the elderly. Part of our dislike for old people is acted out by refusing to give them a diagnosis that we believe to be a birthright of those who are still young. Yet the geriatric patient often has emotional disorders just like the ones younger patients have;

2. against the belief in the possibility of late-age onset of illness. If we make the diagnosis of psychosis, neurosis, or personality disorder at all, we believe the first episode cannot have appeared at such a late date. We insist there must have been an earlier episode. In other words, according to this prejudice, any real emotional illness in the elderly must be chronic, not acute;

3. against the similarity between illnesses of late- and early-age onset. In those rare instances when we admit of late-age onset of illness (paranoia, depression, but rarely mania, and almost never personality disorder), we insist, "It can't be the same disorder." If forced to admit that the disorder is essentially the same, then we resort to insisting that the cause must be different enough to influence the complexion of the illness so as to create what can amount to a distinct disorder. Naturally the provocation for a reactive disorder in the adolescent (loss of a close friend) often seems less momentous than that for the reactive disorder in the elderly where provocations tend to be multiple, cumulative, severe, and permanent, such as loss of one's mate. But the dissimilarities of outcome are probably more apparent than real.

Specific

1. The schizophrenic geriatric patient, whose psychosis is believed untreatable because it is attributed to senility. These patients are often given "small" doses of psychotropics suitable for treating behavioral problems associated with dementia, not the larger doses required for treatment of schizophrenia.

2. The schizoid geriatric patient, whose isolation is not due to dementia but to a personality disorder.

3. The schizotypal geriatric patient, whose stereotyped or peculiar behaviors are not organic perseverations but are mannerisms. (Repetitive manneristic behaviors may also be compulsions.)

4. The paranoid geriatric patient, whose forgetting, for example, of how much money he or she has, is not due to a memory deficit but to a wish to hide money from those whom he or she believes might steal it.

5. The borderline geriatric patient, whose lability is emotional, not due to loss of control as a result of dementia.

6. The passive-dependent geriatric patient, whose inactivity is not due to organic regression or helplessness but to the wish that others will wait on him or her.

7. The passive-aggressive geriatric patient, whose bumbling incapacities (e.g., losing things) are not the result of organic deficit but an expression of stubbornness or covert anger.

8. The depressed geriatric patient, whose depression is not a product of senility but a reaction to loss, among other things, or an introjection of rage when angry, as in other patients who are depressed.

9. The paralyzed obsessional geriatric patient, whose paralytic inability to be spontaneous and make progress results not from early dementing illness but from obsessive uncertainty.

10. The seductive, hysterical geriatric patient: whose inappropriate sexual approaches to members of the opposite sex (often too young) are not due to cortical disinhibition (e.g., frontal lobe) but still living out unresolved Oedipus. (This is the geriatric acting-out equivalent of hysterical acting-out in the younger patient, with one major difference—the younger patient approaches members of the opposite sex not too young but instead too old.)

11. The cyclothymic geriatric patient, whose silly, inappropriate, often impulsive behaviors, are not attributable to frontal-lobe disinhibition but to mood change.

12. The anxious geriatric patient (e.g., catastrophic reactions), whose anxiety and fear are not organically but dynamically determined. In other words, real anxiety and real fear are not the province of the young. For example, forbidden (guilty) hostility or sexuality can create virtually the same response of anxiety in all age groups. In general the geriatric patient has as much to be anxious about or fear from his or her internal and external problems as anyone else—perhaps more.

Treatment Problems

Practical problems

1. Risk-reward ratio. For example, we have the greater risk of side effects from antidepressant medications (dizziness; falling, with fractures; untoward

results of combination with other drugs; and age limitations for the use of some drugs, such as monoamine oxidase inhibitors), plus altered response to these drugs because of the severity and number of losses from these drugs and diminishing personal flexibility.

2. Finances. Medicare and medicaid reimbursement are low and sometimes delayed.

3. Keeping appointments. Interfering here are problems with transportation (especially in bad weather) and intercurrent illnesses.

4. Coexistent medical problems. The nonmedical and medical therapist will want to work closely with an internist.

Deafness is a special problem for the "talking cure." Deafness seems to annoy and bring out sadistic impulses in some therapists at the same time that it creates shame for its bearer.

Countertransference problems

1. Anxiety reaction. Fears about one's own aging and death appear. Too, older patients often make the therapist anxious when they remind the therapist of his or her own parents.

2. Tendency to infantilize. The therapist inspired to baby the older patient will insult, humiliate, and otherwise fail him or her.

3. Impatience and anger. The impatient, angry therapist is often unaware of impatience and anger. Instead, he or she is aware of feeling underpaid, overworked, and underappreciated by these patients and by their families.

4. Pessimism and hopelessness. This is typically acted out by overprescribing drugs that are indicated or by giving drugs when not indicated, or when psychotherapy is to be preferred.

A psychiatrist insisted his depressed patient be given antidepressants, not psychotherapy, though the patient had just lost two friends, was having problems with his wife, and was excessively upset by chest pain and difficulty breathing, diagnosed by the cardiologist as mild cardiac insufficiency.

Transference problems

1. Using age to make the therapist feel helpless or bad. The older patient will use being old and sick to express anger with the therapist. One form of such attack is complaints that are exaggerated, for the purpose of, to quote Jerome Weinberger (personal communication), "beating the therapist over the head with my bloody body." One patient who did this admitted, "I am not as bad off and don't suffer as much as I say I do—for the purpose of upsetting you and getting you mad."

2. Using age as a resistance. The patient will say, "I'm too old to change." As is the case with all resistances, ounces of reality obscure pounds of elaboration.

Family problems

Excessive demands by relatives. The patient's relatives may deal with their (justified and unjustified) guilty anger with the patient by demanding cure, though impossible, and blaming the therapist for poor results, though unavoidable.

Treatment Solutions

Techniques no different from those used for younger patients

The dependent geriatric patient should be pushed, the passive-aggressive geriatric patient told to be a little kinder to those who wish him well, the hypomanic geriatric patient told he or she is excessively high considering his or her circumstances, the depressed geriatric patient confronted with his or her depressive overelaboration of reality and told he or she is excessively low considering his or her circumstances, the obsessional geriatric patient told that an excessive sense of guilt is responsible for an exceptional degree of forward-motion paralysis, and so forth.

Modifications of techniques

1. Modification of goals. Instead of remission the therapist may offer the goal of palliation.

2. Modification of frequency of sessions. Try more frequent sessions after a loss (common in this age group), less frequent sessions when life is stable.

3. Modification of length of sessions. In some elderly patients sessions should be shorter because of their short attention span.

4. More emphasis on physical problems, with drugs and their effects especially important.

5. More emphasis on philosophical and existential matters than on insight. In particular death and dying are matters for philosophical contemplation. A great reliance may be placed on the literature. The therapist may recommend reading material found to be helpful.

6. More emphasis on direction and advice. Blank-screen, purely insight-oriented treatment may not work. The effective therapist is often one with a high-, not a low-, profile philosophy, one who has strong opinions—is even opinionated. A therapist who expresses the feeling that retirement at the age of 65 is bad for you may better be able to help his patients than a therapist who says, "Retirement at 65 works for some but not for others; you decide which is the proper course for you to take, and I'll help you with the decision."

Give advice about such things as the risks as well as the rewards of retirement, about diet (especially low cholesterol and weight loss), and about structuring time.

7. More emphasis on support by others. Recommend that the patient seek peer support with peer identification, activities therapy, pets. Include a special

emphasis on community resource. The community as a resource is as important for the elderly patient as for the young schizophrenic patient.

Dealing with use of age as a resistance

Try dealing with this form of resistance by telling the patient the following:

1. From my experience I know people like you can change.

2. Some disorders in the elderly (some depression, some paranoia) are actually more easily treated than in the young.

3. The older patient has resources the younger patient does not have.

4. How you travel the road is often as important as whether you reach the destination.

5. Time to enjoy it is only one of the rewards of change.

Things not to treat

Depression should be left untreated when desirable, for example, when it is defensive. One patient in a nursing home swathed himself in depression and refused offers of help for the following reasons: he was suffering in this life so that he could better enter heaven; he believed depression appropriate because it meant he loved his departed wife too much to enjoy himself in her absence; and he wanted to save pleasure for later, when he could rejoin his wife after death and share it with her.

Chapter 18

Treating Symptoms with a Physical Caste

PROBLEM

The medical and nonmedical therapist alike should help evaluate, diagnose, treat, and monitor emotional symptoms with a physical caste. These belong to two broad categories: (1) emotional problems presenting as physical symptoms or concerns and (2) physical problems presenting as emotional problems.

SOLUTION

First, learn the different categories of the combined physical-emotional disorder. Second, learn how to evaluate and treat patients from each category.

The Different Categories of Combined Physical-Emotional Disorder

Emotional problems presenting as physical symptoms

The emotional disorders that we can expect to present in a physical way include these:

1. somatoform disorder—hysterical neurosis, conversion type, for example, sensory loss;

2. somatoform disorder—somatization disorder, for example, some head-aches;

3. psychosomatic disorder, for example, some cases of asthma, ulcers;

4. depression, where depression presents not only as a disorder of mood but also as depressive *equivalents* (symptoms such as headache, back pain) or as depressive *vegetative symptoms* (headaches, constipation, insomnia);

5. anxiety, where anxiety presents with somatic manifestations, such as light-headedness, diarrhea, weakness, dizziness, and feeling faint.

Emotional problems presenting as physical concerns

1. Hypochondriasis, when obsession with or delusion about physical illness creates worry out of nothing or elaborates a minor physical sensation, such as normal twitching, or a minor physical problem, such as arthritis.

2. Post-traumatic stress disorder, when the original and thus the repeating trauma have a somatic implication. For example, if the original trauma was a surgical procedure such as a tonsillectomy, the recurrences of the traumatic episode might have such physical aspects as feeling floaty (from anesthesia memory) or tightness of the throat.

Physical problems presenting as emotional problems

Examples include thyrotoxicosis presenting as anxiety or depression; vitamin deficiencies presenting as acute psychosis; central nervous system lesions pre-senting as hysterical neurosis, conversion type; frontal-lobe syndrome (for ex-ample, due to multiple sclerosis) presenting as mania; senile dementia presenting as paranoia, depression, or impulse disorder; and epilepsy presenting as an obsessive-compulsive disorder (when seizures take the form of repeated words or short phrases).

Debatable physical-emotional relationships

An example is chronic fatigue syndrome, where it is unclear if physical prob-lems cause emotional problems or the other way around.

Physical complications of psychiatric illness

SELF-INDUCED

Examples include complications, such as venereal disease, of sexual acting-out due to an impulse disorder, hysterical personality disorder, or psychopathy; complications of an eating disorder such as overeating, undereating, bulimic episodes, cardiac irregularities from low potassium; self-damage due to a self-destructive factitious disorder; and self-damage due to suicidal behavior.

INDUCED BY ANOTHER

Nonphysician. This includes injury to victims of abuse, rape, and attempted or effected homicide.

Physician. Of special note are reactions to psychotropic drugs, of which there are two categories:

1. Drug side effects. These effects, while physically caused, can be mistaken for psychological. Examples include impotence from antidepressants, feelings of detachment from phenothiazines.

2. Drug interactions. These interactions, while physically caused, can be mistaken for psychological. Examples include the interaction of monoamine oxidase inhibitors with the tricyclic antidepressants (also foods such as red wine and cheese), and possibly the interaction of haloperidol with lithium.

Physical-emotional complexes that are normal or variations of normal

This might include some premenstrual tension syndromes and some mild postpartum blues.

Emotional reactions to medical concerns or conditions

An example is reactive depression brought on by heart attack, cancer, or any fatal illness.

How to Treat

The nonmedical therapist's approach

The nonmedical therapist should not be made to feel that he or she is practicing medicine without a license simply because he or she shows interest in the patient's medical well-being. The nonmedical therapist, like the medical therapist, is expected to make a differential diagnosis of physical symptoms with an emotional basis and of emotional symptoms with a physical basis. There is, however, a difference: the nonmedical therapist should not be expected to know all the possibilities, nor should he or she be expected to make the final diagnostic decision. This is the province of others, such as an internist or a psychiatrist.

Rule: Never be alone, without specialized medical help, in evaluating or treating a patient with physical complaints.

Rule: Always consider as insufficient simple assurances from the patient that he or she is all right physically. Get it in writing from the treating internist, family physician, or other practitioner.

There are other conditions, such as suicidal or homicidal behavior, that, while not physical in the narrow sense of the term, require the presence of a physician if only because it is the physician who has the most emergency room experience and has admitting privileges to the psychiatric hospital.

The psychiatrist's approach

THE PHYSICAL EXAMINATION DONE BY A PSYCHIATRIST

Except for examination of the pudendal region, the laying on of hands by the psychiatrist is not per se too overwhelming, intrusive, or sexual. The psychiatrist who performs a blood pressure reading, eye examination, and the like on appropriate patients will not be overstepping the boundaries of good taste or good psychiatric management or necessarily creating unresolvable transference problems. And the psychiatrist who routinely believes he or she should not perform *any* part of the physical examination is in some observers' opinion no different from the psychologist who feels he or she should *never* debase or insult the patient, or interfere with the transference, by performing psychological testing. (However, common sense and medicolegal considerations beyond the scope of this text limit the role of the psychiatrist as primary medical physician.)

THE NEUROPSYCHIATRIC EXAMINATION

Because the organic parameters (e.g., memory) of mental status testing can embarrass the patient, infantilize him or her, or seem at best peripheral and at worst inappropriate, the psychiatrist will have to use good judgment in deciding whether to include mental status questions in the initial or subsequent evaluation. Ask yourself if you should ask a possibly intact patient a question such as, How much is 100 − 7, and 7 from that? Fortunately, in many instances the patient's general neuropsychiatric health can be divined without such special testing. However, the psychiatrist who has a question about possible organic disorder can, after a suitable apology, feel free to administer necessary mental status test questions, though potentially insulting. The judicious selection of test questions is of as much importance as the decision to test or not to test. Hint: Such tests for memory as three objects after a few minutes will be more palatable than such overly elementary questions as, what is today's date?

DOING A PSYCHIATRIC CONSULTATION

Here are some of the things the good psychiatric consultant does:

1. The good psychiatric consultant answers yes, no, maybe, or I don't know to questions asked; avoids answering questions that are not asked; and avoids speculation on matters unlikely to be of interest to medical personnel (such as some Freudian dynamics).

2. The good psychiatric consultant is aware that the nonpsychiatric physician calls as often for personal as for medical support—a kind of crisis intervention, for him- or herself, or for the ward personnel (nurses, social workers) involved with the patient. Often the medical physician or nurses say they feel perplexed medically but actually feel personally helpless, and ashamed of their helplessness, or feel angry, and guilty about their anger. Because they are uncomfortable about expressing these feelings, they ask instead about the patient.

3. The good psychiatric consultant can help most by distancing him- or herself and giving an overview. Those primarily responsible for the patient are often too involved and so cannot see the forest for the trees. For this reason, some of the simplest consultations can be the best.

Example. One patient had a skin ulcer on her leg. Repeated grafts failed for reasons unknown. The patient was anxious and depressed, which was believed to be the result of the repeated sloughing of the graft. A psychiatric consultation was obtained. The psychiatrist made the following simple pronouncement: This patient is rubbing off her skin, giving herself a new ulcer; put on an Unna's boot (a plaster protective covering like a cast).

Even that did not do any good. The psychiatrist, called again, realized that "she is opening a coat hanger and inserting it between the boot and the skin, then rubbing the skin off." He recommended 24–hour nursing observation. The ulcer healed.

4. Teach others how to use the consultant (described below).

The nonpsychiatric physician's approach

ASKING FOR A CONSULTATION

The nonpsychiatric physician should call for a consultation not only for help with a management problem, to determine suicidal or homicidal risk, or to determine competency to sign for surgery, but also for differential diagnosis, to make a treatment plan should the patient's illness turn out to be purely psychiatric (Munchausen's Syndrome schizophrenia), and/or to participate in treatment planning should the patient's illness be a physical illness of possible emotional cause (some asthma, ulcerative colitis), or should there be emotional consequences of the patient's physical illness (cardiac illness with associated depression). In other words, the nonpsychiatric physician should ask for a consultation that involves the therapist's expertise at every step in evaluation, diagnosis, and treatment.

Selected Bibliography

RECOMMENDED READINGS

Abraham, Karl. *Clinical Papers and Essays on Psycho-Analysis*. New York: Basic Books, 1955 vol. 2.

Agras, W. Stewart, and Robert Berkowitz. Behavior therapy. In John A. Talbott, Robert E. Hales, and Stuart C. Yudofsky (eds.), *Textbook of Psychiatry*. Washington, D.C.: American Psychiatric Press, Inc., 1988.

American Psychiatric Association. *Diagnostic and Statistical Manual of Mental Disorders*, 3d ed., revised. Washington, D.C.: American Psychiatric Association, 1987.

———. *Treatment of Psychiatric Disorders*. Washington, D.C.: American Psychiatric Association, 1989.

Beck, Aaron T. *Cognitive Therapy and the Emotional Disorders*. New York: International Universities Press, 1976.

Bellak, Leopold. *Disorders of the Schizophrenic Syndrome*. New York: Basic Books, 1979.

Berne, Eric. *Games People Play*. New York: Grove Press, 1964.

Bibring, Edward. The mechanism of depression. In Phyllis Greenacre (ed.), *Affective Disorders*. New York: International Universities Press, 1953.

Bonime, Walter. Depression as a practice: dynamic and psychotherapeutic considerations. *Comprehensive Psychiat.*, 1: 194–198 (1960).

Brenner, Charles. *An Elementary Textbook of Psychoanalysis*. New York: International Universities Press, 1955.

Cleckley, Hervey. *The Mask of Sanity*. St. Louis: C. V. Mosby, 1955.

Colby, Kenneth Mark. *A Primer for Psychotherapists*. New York: Ronald Press, 1951.

Fenichel, Otto. *Problems of Psychoanalytic Technique*. Albany, NY: The Psychoanalytic Quarterly: Albany, 1941.

Freud, Anna. *The Ego and the Mechanisms of Defense*. New York: International Universities Press, 1946.

Freud, Sigmund. Analysis of a phobia in a five-year-old boy. In James Strachey (ed.), *Standard Edition of the Complete Psychological Works of Sigmund Freud*, vol. 14. London: Hogarth Press, 1955.

————. Fragment of an analysis of a case of hysteria. In James Strachey (ed.), *Standard Edition of Complete Psychological Works of Sigmund Freud*, vol. 7. London: Hogarth Press, 1953.

————. *The Interpretation of Dreams*. New York: Basic Books, 1959.

————. Introductory lectures on psycho-analysis. In James Strachey (ed.), *Standard Edition of Complete Psychological Works of Sigmund Freud*, vols. 15 and 16. London: Hogarth Press, 1961 and 1963.

————. Mourning and melancholia. In James Strachey (ed.), *Standard Edition of Complete Psychological Works of Sigmund Freud*, vol. 14. London: Hogarth Press, 1957.

————. Notes upon a case of obsessional neurosis. In James Strachey (ed.), *Standard Edition of Complete Psychological Works of Sigmund Freud*, vol. 10. London: Hogarth Press, 1955.

————. *The Problem of Anxiety*. New York: The Psychoanalytic Quarterly Press and W. W. Norton, 1936.

————. Psycho-analytic notes on an autobiographical account of a case of paranoia (dementia paranoides). In James Strachey (ed.), *Standard Edition of Complete Psychological Works of Sigmund Freud*, vol. 12. London: Hogarth Press, 1958.

————. Some character-types met with in psycho-analytic work. In James Strachey (ed.), *Standard Edition of Complete Psychological Works of Sigmund Freud*, vol. 14. London: Hogarth Press, 1957.

————. Three essays on the theory of sexuality. In James Strachey (ed.), *Standard Edition of Complete Psychological Works of Sigmund Freud*, vol. 7. London: Hogarth Press, 1953.

Fromm-Reichmann, Freida. *Principles of Intensive Psychotherapy*. Chicago: The University of Chicago Press, 1960.

Gill, Merton, Richard Newman, and Fredrick C. Redlich. *The Initial Interview In Psychiatric Practice*. New York: International Universities Press, 1954.

Gray, Sheila Hafter. Brief psychotherapy: a development approach. *Journal of the Philadelphia Association of Psychoanalysis*, 5: 29–36 (1978).

Haley, Jay. *Problem-Solving Therapy*. San Francisco: Jossey-Bass, 1976.

Hendrick, Ives. *Facts and Theories of Psychoanalysis*. New York: Alfred A. Knopf, 1958.

Hill, Lewis B. *Psychotherapeutic Intervention in Schizophrenia*. Chicago: The University of Chicago Press, 1955.

Horner, Althea. *Treating the Oedipal Patient in Brief Psychotherapy*. New York: Aronson, 1985.

Kantor, Martin. *Determining Mental Status: The "Physical Examination" of Psychiatry*. Springfield, Illinois: Charles C. Thomas, 1988.

———. (In preparation.) *Diagnosis and Treatment of the Personality Disorders.*

Kernberg, Otto F. *Borderline Conditions and Pathological Narcissism.* New York: Jason Aronson, 1975.

Kohut, Heinz J. *The Analysis of the Self.* New York: International Universities Press, 1971.

———. *The Restoration of the Self.* New York: International Universities Press, 1977.

Lindemann, Erich. Symptomatology and management of acute grief. *Am. J. Psychiatry,* 101: 141–148, 1944.

MacKinnon, Roger A., and Robert Michels. *The Psychiatric Interview in Clinical Practice.* Philadelphia: W. B. Saunders, 1971.

Meissner, William W. Theories of personality and psychopathology: classical psychoanalysis. In Harold I. Kaplan and Benjamin J. Sadock (eds.), *Comprehensive Textbook of Psychiatry/IV.* Baltimore: Williams and Wilkins, 1985.

Miller, Laura J. Inpatient management of borderline personality disorder: a review and update. *Journal of Personality Disorders,* 3 (2): 122–134 (1989).

Millon, Theodore. *Disorders of Personality: DSM III Axis II.* New York: John Wiley & Sons, Inc., 1981.

Modell, Arnold H. Primitive object relationships and the predisposition to schizophrenia. *Int. J. Psychoanal.,* 44: 282–291 (1963).

Nemiah, John C. Phobic disorders (phobic neuroses). In Harold I. Kaplan and Benjamin J. Sadock (eds.), *Comprehensive Textbook of Psychiatry/IV.* Baltimore: Williams and Wilkins, 1985.

Pinsker, Henry. Supportive therapy. (Grand Rounds presentations at Beth Israel and at St. Vincent's Hospital, New York City, January 1988.)

Rado, Sandor. Obsessive behavior. In Silvano Arieti (ed.), *American Handbook of Psychiatry,* vol. 1. New York: Basic Books, 1959.

Reich, Wilhelm. *Character-Analysis.* New York: Orgone Institute Press, 1949.

Sederer, Lloyd I., and Jane Thorbeck. First do no harm: short-term inpatient psychotherapy of the borderline patient. *Hospital and Community Psychiatry,* 37 (7): 692–696 (1986).

Sifneos, Peter. *Short-Term Dynamic Psychotherapy.* New York: Plenum, 1979.

Sullivan, Harry Stack. *The Psychiatric Interview.* New York: W. W. Norton, 1954.

Swenson, Charles, et al. Two approaches to the borderline patient. *Journal of Personality Disorders,* 3 (1): 26–35 (1989).

Tarachow, Sidney. *An Introduction to Psychotherapy.* New York: International Universities Press, 1963.

Thigpen, Corbett, and Hervey Cleckley. *The Three Faces of Eve.* New York: McGraw-Hill, 1957.

Webb, Linda J., et al. (eds.) *DSM-III Training Guide.* New York: Brunner/Mazel, 1981.

Weinberger, J. L. "Basic Concepts in Diagnosis and Treatment of Borderline States" in *Ego Psychology and Dynamic Casework, Papers from the Smith College of Social Work,* pp. 111–116, edited by Howard J. Parad, Family Service Association of America, 1958.

———. A triad of silence: silence, masochism, and depression. *International J. of Psychoanalysis,* 45:304–308 (1964).

Widiger, Thomas A., et al. The DSM-III-R personality disorders: an overview. *Am. J. Psychiatry,* 145: 786–795 (1988).

Winnicott, Donald. W. Transitional objects and transitional phenomena. *Int. J. Psychoanal.,* 34:89–97 (1953).

Winston, Arnold, Henry Pinsker, and Leigh McCullough. A review of supportive psychotherapy. *Hospital and Community Psychiatry*, 37 (11): 1,105–1,114 (1986).

Wolberg, Lewis R. *The Technique of Psychotherapy*. New York: Grune & Stratton, 1954.

Zetzel, Elizabeth. A developmental approach to the borderline patient. *Am. J. Psychiatry*, 127: 867–871 (1971).

SUPPLEMENTAL READINGS

Abraham, Karl. A short study of the development of the libido. In *Clinical Papers and Essays on Psycho-Analysis*, vol 1. New York: Basic Books, 1955.

Adler, Gerald. Psychotherapy of the narcissistic personality disorder patient: two contrasting approaches. *Am. J. Psychiatry*, 143: 430–436 (1986).

Bemporad, Jules R., and Henry Pinsker. Schizophrenia: the manifest symptomatology. In Silvano Arieti and Eugene B. Brody (eds.), *American Handbook of Psychiatry*, 2d ed., vol. 3. New York: Basic Books, 1974.

Brody, Silvia. Psychoanalytic theories of infant development and its disturbances: a critical evaluation. *The Psychoanalytic Quarterly*, 51: 526–597 (1982).

Cameron, Norman. Paranoid conditions and paranoia. In Silvano Arieti (ed.), *American Handbook of Psychiatry*, vol. 1. New York: Basic Books, 1959.

Cancro, Robert. Overview of affective disorders. In Harold I. Kaplan and Benjamin J. Sadock (eds.), *Comprehensive Textbook of Psychiatry/IV*. Baltimore: Williams and Wilkins, 1985.

Davis, Glenn C., and Akiskal, Hagop S. Descriptive, biological, and theoretical aspects of borderline personality disorder. *Hospital and Community Psychiatry*, 37(7): 685–691 (1986).

Federn, Paul. *Ego Psychology and the Psychoses*. New York: Basic Books, 1952.

Fenichel, Otto. *The Psychoanalytic Theory of Neurosis*. New York: W. W. Norton, 1945.

Ferenczi, Sandor. *Sex in Psycho-analysis*. New York: Dover Publications, 1956.

Freud, Sigmund. Character and anal erotism. In James Strachey (ed.), *Standard Edition of Complete Psychological Works of Sigmund Freud*, vol. 19. London: Hogarth Press, 1959.

———. The economic problem of masochism. In James Strachey (ed.), *Standard Edition of Complete Psychological Works of Sigmund Freud*, vol. 19. London: Hogarth Press, 1961.

———. On narcissism: an introduction [1914]. In Alix and James Strachey (trans.), *Collected Papers*, vol. 4. London: Hogarth Press and the Institute of Psychoanalysis, 1957.

———. Some neurotic mechanisms in jealousy, paranoia and homosexuality. In James Strachey (ed.), *Standard Edition of Complete Psychological Works of Sigmund Freud*, vol. 18. London: Hogarth Press, 1955.

Ginsberg, George L. Psychiatric history and mental status examination. In Harold I. Kaplan and Benjamin J. Sadock (eds.), *Comprehensive Textbook of Psychiatry/IV*. Baltimore: Williams and Wilkins, 1985.

Giovacchini, Peter The psychoanalytic treatment of alienated patients. In James Masterson (ed.), *New Perspectives on Psychotherapy of the Borderline Adult*. New York: Brunner/Mazel, 1978.

Gray, Sheila Hafter. Developmental issues in young adulthood. (Paper presented before American Society for Adolescent Psychiatry, in press.)

————. The resolution of the Oedipus complex in women. *Journal of the Philadelphia Association for Psychoanalysis,* 111 (4): 103–111 (1976).

Greenacre, Phyllis. *Trauma, Growth, and Personality.* New York: W. W. Norton, 1952.

Grinker, Roy R., Sr., Beatrice Werble, and Robert C. Drye. *The Borderline Syndrome.* New York: Basic Books, 1968.

Gunderson, John G. *Borderline Personality Disorder.* Washington, D.C.: American Psychiatric Press, 1984.

————. DSM-III diagnosis of personality disorders. In J. Frosch (ed.), *Current Perspectives on Personality Disorders.* Washington, D.C.: American Psychiatric Press, 1983.

Gunderson, John G., and Glen R. Elliott. The interface between borderline personality disorder and affective disorder. *Am. J. Psychiatry,* 142: 277–288 (1985).

Hoch, Paul H., and Phillip Polatin. Pseudoneurotic forms of schizophrenia. *Psychiatr. Quart.,* 23: 248–276 (1949).

Horowitz, Mardi J. Stress-response syndromes: a review of posttraumatic and adjustment disorders. *Hospital and Community Psychiatry,* 37(3): 241–249 (1986).

Kardiner, Abram. Traumatic neuroses of war. In Silvano Arieti (ed.), *American Handbook of Psychiatry,* vol. 1. New York: Basic Books, 1959.

Kolb, Lawrence C. *Modern Clinical Psychiatry,* 9th ed. Philadelphia: W. B. Saunders, 1977.

Laughlin, Henry P. *The Neuroses in Clinical Practice.* Philadelphia: W. B. Saunders, 1956.

Lewin, Bertram O. *The Psychoanalysis of Elation.* New York: W. W. Norton, 1950.

Linn, Louis. Clinical manifestations of psychiatric disorders. In Kaplan, Harold I., and Benjamin J. Sadock (eds.), *Comprehensive Textbook of Psychiatry/IV.* Baltimore: Williams and Wilkins, 1985.

Lion, John R. *Personality Disorders: Diagnosis and Management,* 2d ed. Baltimore: Williams & Wilkins, 1981.

Mahler, Margaret S. Thoughts about development and individuation. *Psychoanalytic Study of the Child,* 18: 307–324 (1963).

Masterson, James F. *The Narcissistic and Borderline Disorders.* New York: Brunner/Mazel, 1981.

Meissner, William W. *The Borderline Spectrum: Differential Diagnosis and Developmental Issues.* New York: Aronson, 1984.

Pope, Harrison G., Jr. Distinguishing bipolar disorder from schizophrenia in clinical practice: guidelines and case reports. *Hospital and Community Psychiatry,* 34(4): 322–328 (1983).

Rank, Otto. *The Trauma of Birth.* New York: Robert Brunner, 1952.

Sadock, Virginia. Psychosexual dysfunctions and treatment. In Harold I. Kaplan and Benjamin J. Sadock (eds.), *Comprehensive Textbook of Psychiatry/IV.* Baltimore: Williams and Wilkins, 1985.

Salzman, Leon, and Frank H. Thaler. Obsessive-compulsive disorders: a review of the literature. *Am. J. Psychiatry,* 138: 286–296 (1981).

Selye, Hans. *The Stress of Life.* New York: McGraw-Hill, 1956.

Shainess, Natalie. Masochism—or self-defeating personality? *J. Personality Disorders,* 1: 174–177 (1987).

Spitz, Rene A. Anaclitic depression. *Psychoanalytic Study of the Child,* 2: 313–342 (1946).

Stanton, Alfred H. Personality disorders. In Armand M. Nicholi, Jr. (ed.), *The Harvard Guide to Modern Psychiatry*. Cambridge: Harvard University Press, 1978.

Strauss, John S., and William T. Carpenter, Jr. *Schizophrenia*. New York: Plenum, 1981.

Sullivan, Harry Stack. *The Interpersonal Theory of Psychiatry*. New York: W. W. Norton, 1953.

Svrakic, Dragan M. Emotional features of narcissistic personality disorder. *Am. J. Psychiatry*, 142: 720–724 (1985).

Thetford, William N., and Roger Walsh. Theories of personality and psychopathology: schools derived from psychology and philosophy. In Harold I. Kaplan and Benjamin J. Sadock (eds.), *Comprehensive Textbook of Psychiatry/IV*. Baltimore: Williams and Wilkins, 1985.

Weinberger, Jerome L., and Martin Kantor. Possible sequelae of trauma and somatic disorder in early life. *Intl. J. Psychiatry in Medicine*, 7(4): 337–350 (1976–1977).

Index

ABOUT THE AUTHOR

MARTIN KANTOR, M.D., received his medical degree from Harvard University and his residency training in psychiatry at Massachusetts General Hospital and Stanford University Medical Center. He is the author of *Determining Mental Status: The "Physical Examination" of Psychiatry* (1988) and has coauthored journal articles on post-traumatic stress disorder and the musical expression of psychopathology. He is currently in private practice in New York and Bay Head, New Jersey, and is consulting psychiatrist on the staff of the Medical Center of Ocean County, New Jersey. His past teaching appointments include attending psychiatrist at Massachusetts General Hospital and assistant clinical professor of psychiatry at Mount Sinai Medical School.